"This is the ideal book for those looking to peek behind the curtain of how films are actually financed and therefore completed. A must read for independent producers and filmmakers."
– **Josh Ellis,** *Professor at Miami Dade College*

Independent Film Finance

For aspiring producers and directors who need to learn film finance from the ground up, this revolutionary new book teaches the fundamentals, through the voices of more than 60 successful independent producers. Using a research and data-based approach, award-winning professor David Offenberg combines the wisdom of well-known and successful producers into one fun, easy-to-follow guide.

Within, readers will learn how to talk to potential investors and what those financiers will expect from them in return. The book is also packed with informative anecdotes and examples to enrich each chapter and contextualize the film financing landscape. As the book progresses, equity, debt, revenue, profits, and their role in your movie will be explored. Accessible information about tax incentives and profit participations is included to help emerging filmmakers build out a workable financing plan. The book combines hard numbers and data sets, with direct guidance from successful producers, to construct a holistic overview on how you can turn your new-found financial knowledge into funding for your movie.

This ground-breaking book is a must-read for any aspiring producer or director who wishes to gain an informed and easily digestible understanding of film finance.

David Offenberg is an Associate Professor of Finance in the College of Business Administration at Loyola Marymount University in Los Angeles, and is amongst the world's leading academic experts in entertainment finance. Dr. Offenberg won the most prestigious teaching award for finance professors in 2018 and the Financial Management Association's Innovation in Teaching Award. He is frequently quoted in the press, with mentions by CNBC, *The Hollywood Reporter*, NPR, *Vanity Fair*, *Wall St. Journal*, and *The Wrap*.

Independent Film Finance

A Research-Based Guide to Funding Your Movie

David Offenberg

NEW YORK AND LONDON

Designed cover image: © Fanatic Studio / Alamy Stock Photo

First published 2024
by Routledge
605 Third Avenue, New York, NY 10158

and by Routledge
4 Park Square, Milton Park, Abingdon, Oxon, OX14 4RN

Routledge is an imprint of the Taylor & Francis Group, an informa business

© 2024 David Offenberg

The right of David Offenberg to be identified as author of this work has been asserted in accordance with sections 77 and 78 of the Copyright, Designs and Patents Act 1988.

All rights reserved. No part of this book may be reprinted or reproduced or utilised in any form or by any electronic, mechanical, or other means, now known or hereafter invented, including photocopying and recording, or in any information storage or retrieval system, without permission in writing from the publishers.

Trademark notice: Product or corporate names may be trademarks or registered trademarks, and are used only for identification and explanation without intent to infringe.

ISBN: 978-1-032-42604-4 (hbk)
ISBN: 978-1-032-42605-1 (pbk)
ISBN: 978-1-003-36344-6 (ebk)

DOI: 10.4324/9781003363446

Typeset in Sabon
by Apex CoVantage, LLC

To my wife

To my daughter

To my son

Contents

Acknowledgments	xi
Introduction	1
Part 1: Business and Finance Basics	5
1 The Wisdom of the Crowd	7
2 The (Movie) Business	13
3 The Language of Business	25
4 Debt Financing	39
5 Participation and Deferred Compensation	50
6 Tax Incentives and Soft Money	61
7 Budgets	72
8 Four Paths to Funding Your Budget	78
Part 2: Financing Your Film	83
9 First Law of Film Finance	85
10 The Market Value of Your Film	89
11 A Financing Plan	110
12 Equity in Independent Film	127

Contents

Part 3: Beyond the Basics — 147

13 Experience Matters — 149

14 People Matter — 156

15 Pipelines Matter — 164

16 Luck Matters — 167

17 Many Other Things Matter Too — 170

18 Action Plan — 179

Appendix: Additional Resources — 181
Glossary — 183
Index — 186

Acknowledgments

I owe so much gratitude to the people who made this book possible. In particular, I need to thank Rosanne Korenberg. She was my first interview, and has been there for me ever since. I owe a ton of gratitude to the producers who made this book possible. They are all named in the first chapter.

This book is much better because of editing from Brandon Katz, my wife, Kimberly Offenberg, and my father, Lawrence Offenberg. I received helpful introductions and guidance from executives, attorneys, & financiers including Tony Beaudoin, Tiffany Boyle, Marco Cordova, Grady Craig, Nick Dang, Matt Feil, Peter Graham, Chris Howland, Peter Klass, Trea Lachowicz, Lex McNaughton, Blake Pickens, Tom Sheppard, Amy Taylor, Peter Wetherell, and Jonathon Wolf. Additional background information was kindly provided by Brian Beckmann, Jason Kummer, Andrea Scarso, and Viviana Zarragoitia.

I appreciate the academicians who supported me on this journey. Jason Squire has been an excellent mentor to me. I received terrific feedback from Josh Ellis and Tim O'Hair. I applaud advice from Avri Ravid on the statistics and Heather Silber-Mohammed on the publishing process. I appreciate support from my colleagues usan Elkinawy, Larry Kalbers, Josh Spizman, and my assistant, Dionne Scrivens. I received exceptional research help from Akshay Pansare and Wendy Xu. Work on this book was completed during my sabbatical in 2021, thanks to the support of the Office of the Provost of LMU.

Special thanks to the exceptional team at Routledge, including Dan Kershaw and Genni Eccles.

Introduction

> I had to learn finance as a matter of survival.
> – John Baldecchi, producer

I am as guilty as anyone in this business. I organized finance panels to help young filmmakers learn how to raise money for their projects, and then listened to one successful producer after another explain how they raise money, now that they are successful and carry a full Rolodex. *Find a studio that wants to help you. Just go talk to the people at Netflix. Reach out to the wealthiest people in your network.* It was not helpful to the audience.

I decided to go back, way back to the beginning of their careers, to understand what these producers did to get their first film made, besides relying on luck. I decided to set aside anecdotes and gather the data to determine what these successful producers have in common.

Data is the lifeblood of our modern world. It is how SpaceX lands rockets standing upright, based on thousands of measurements per second about its movements and systems. It is how your credit card company knows your card has been stolen, based on your past purchasing behavior. It is why Netflix offers me *The Umbrella Academy* and offers you *Mindhunters*, based on our watch history.

The beauty of data, the reason that I love data, is because it boils away lots of randomness and allows us to see common patterns. It separates out the lucky experiences from the meaningful experiences in the careers of the producers that I interviewed. This book is built on data, so you can use the insights from my data to help you make better choices.[1]

The data used to write this book has never been collected before, and it is magnificent! There are so many great things to learn from it. To give you a sneak peek, the total lifetime box office for all of the independent producers interviewed for this book exceeds $1.8 billion (excluding films that they executive produced). They have collectively produced over 450 films. Their films won every major award, from the Oscars on down. The data reveals the smart choices that they made to grow successful careers.

DOI: 10.4324/9781003363446-1

Don't get me wrong, some producers were kissed by extraordinary luck. A stranger worth millions snuck onto Andrew van den Houten's set in New York City, just to see what was going on, and became an investor. Oliver Stone showed up to Janet Yang's film festival and eventually hired her, before she ever produced *The Joy Luck Club*. (Of course, Ms. Yang is an exceptional talent, as confirmed by her election as president of the Academy of Motion Picture Arts and Sciences in 2022.) Vera Farmiga offered to direct *Higher Ground* for Carly Hugo and Matthew Parker after the original director dropped out. Judd Payne is very clear that he feels lucky to have worked with the Russo brothers (directors of *Avengers: Infinity War*) on *Cherry*. Luck happens.

For the rest of your career, you will hear stories about producers who were lucky. They are great tales, but they are the basis of awful advice. Please do not build your career based on dreams of good fortune. This book provides you with guidance, based on data, to help you make smart choices that improve the chances of getting your films made. In the words of producer Brad Zions, you will still need to "scrap and scrape to do it the indie way," but you will have the tools to approach your scrapping and scraping better.

* * *

The goal of this book is to teach you the basics of independent film finance. At the heart of it is a new, simple First Law of Film Finance that will be introduced to you in the middle of the book. It says that:

Market Value > Financing Plan > Budget

In plain English, the way to ensure that your film is a financial success is for the market value to be bigger than the financing plan, and for the financing plan to be bigger than the budget. To truly appreciate these truths, you need a reasonable understanding of the basics of finance inside and outside of the independent film business. The early chapters will give you that foundation, and then the later chapters will guide you in implementing this law.

I offer many anecdotes and quotes in this book, to give you something concrete to grasp, but almost never as an example of the one time this happened in the history of film. With most of the stories I share, I could change the name of the producer and the title of the film, and the rest of the story would still hold. I do not mean to take anything away from the folks that I quoted. I spent up to two hours interviewing some of these producers, and have pages and pages of notes from each of them. If I included all of the great quotes and stories, I would have a ridiculously repetitive book. Lucky for you, there are genuinely common themes within the wisdom shared by these successful producers.

If you are wondering, I am not a producer. To the best of my knowledge, I am the world's only tenured finance professor in this field, I've written the book on it (this one!), and I won the world's most prestigious teaching award in finance. For the purposes of writing this book, being a scholar instead of a producer carries a real advantage. I do not have any biases built in because of "how I did it" or the luck that blessed me. The advice that I can offer you is the wisdom of the crowd, shaped through the lens of my career teaching finance. Along those lines, I hope that you do not feel like this book is too preachy. Throughout, I'm condensing hundreds of pieces of advice from many successful producers and trying to make all of it manageable. Even though I don't always attribute the specific guidance to a specific producer, virtually every bit of counsel is coming from someone other than me.

* * *

Early in my wife's first pregnancy, we started hearing the horror stories and learning so many things that could go wrong in the months and years to come. There were definitely moments of *what have we gotten into??* Nonetheless, learning, preparing, baby-proofing, saving for college, and everything else that we did to get ready was time well-spent. When our baby arrived, there were many experiences we were unprepared for, but the preparations helped shift an unbearably overwhelming experience to something bearably overwhelming.

Similarly, there will be a few horror stories in the pages to come. I don't sugar-coat things. My hope is that you walk into the process of financing your first film with your eyes wide open, not with blinders on. The more you know, the better prepared you will be. As you read this book, you may come to a point where you are feeling discouraged, because producing is really hard and there is so much to learn. In those moments, I hope that you will remember that there are thousands of successful independent film producers around the world. Lots of people make a career out of producing, and new movies get greenlit every single day. You can do this!

Every single producer that I interviewed talked comfortably about the math behind their films. There is going to be a little bit of elementary school math in this book because it is necessary. Finance inherently involves numbers that must be added, subtracted, and turned into percentages, so you must be comfortable with numbers to become a successful producer. Unlike elementary school, mistakes with the numbers on films have real consequences (i.e. lawsuits and bankruptcies). The good news is that you should never need to do more than simple math – add, subtract, find a percentage, and take an average. (Or you can let Google Sheets do that math for you.)

Getting through the math and the tougher stories will take a bit of persistence. You can think of this as your first test as an independent filmmaker. Every single one of the producers that I spoke with showed a tremendous amount of persistence throughout their career. It is the most important personality trait anyone would need to raise the money for a movie.

There is a glossary in the back. I suggest that you put a bookmark or paperclip now so that you can flip back and forth. There is a lot of terminology in this book that may be new to you, and having quick access to the glossary will help you get through it.

As a college professor, I give out failing grades from time-to-time. Never happily, never without lots of thought and reflection, but it happens. The students who fail my classes are usually getting a message that finance is not the right career path for them, and they need to find something that is a better fit. The earlier they figure that out, the better. Very often, they pick another major, graduate, and go on to have a successful career in another field.

I am saying this because I know that some readers will hit the harder parts of this book and feel very discouraged. Finance is not for everyone. Raising money is a tough job. In reading this book, if you find that the finance side of the business is not for you, then that is a win. You just need to build exceptionally strong skills in another part of the producing process, so that you can add value to your financially-savvy producing partners. Your strengths might lie in attaching talent or finding and developing stories instead, and those are critical roles too.

* * *

My friend and colleague Rosanne Korenberg still remembers the day she learned that her first film, *Hard Candy*, would be financed. When I asked how she felt in that moment, she simply said, "I was elated!" I hope this book provides you with the tools to get you to that point of elation too.

Note

1 Data is also the reason this book has a boring but easy-to-discover title. I really wanted to call it "Ask Your Rich Uncle (and Other Research-Based Advice for Financing Your First Film)," but the search algorithms would never recommend it with that title.

Part 1
Business and Finance Basics

1 The Wisdom of the Crowd

> It's a producer's job to find out what the market wants.
> – Matthew Rhodes, producer

Nicholas Tabarrok had worked on sets as a production manager and line producer for about four years, and then decided it was time to produce his first film, *Motel*. Back then, in 1997, he did not know anyone who could help him finance his project. He was starting from scratch. A friend from high school introduced him to an entertainment lawyer. It seemed like a helpful introduction, but Mr. Tabarrok had never worked with an attorney before, and did not know what to expect. It so happened that this lawyer had deep connections with the Canadian entertainment company Telescene. They read the *Motel* script and agreed to finance the film in a matter of weeks. Mr. Tabarrok told me:

> They would send checks as I needed them. I'd say I need a hundred grand this week, and here came a hundred grand. I told them I needed 250 the next, and here came [$250,000]. I didn't know how rare and unusual [that was], and how lucky I had it.

Lucky! Absolutely! I tell you this story because I want to get the golden elephant out of the room. What happened to Mr. Tabarrok can happen and has happened, but it's extremely rare. If you go into your career expecting to get lucky, you will probably wait a lifetime. You will almost certainly not get to skip straight to the end of your film financing journey. The chances of your movie being fully financed by the first person to read your script are very, very, very small. It happened to only two producers out of the 50 that I interviewed, and both of those were back in the 1990s, when VHS ruled the world. Times have changed. Believe me, times have changed.

Mr. Tabarrok got to skip virtually all of the tedious, disappointing steps in financing an independent film, and somehow got to jump straight to the end. He will tell you that he missed out on learning any number of important lessons that come with financing your first film, and he "had to be disabused of that notion, and realize that it's much harder than that." None of his later films were financed so easily.

To get to the place where you are ready to ask investors for money, you need to understand some finance basics, and some fundamentals about how the movie business works. With the help and advice from dozens of successful producers – the wisdom of the crowd – I will get you to that starting line competently.

I interviewed the producers featured in this book in 2021 and 2022. Throughout the book, I might call them my producers, my interview subjects, and, if I am feeling particularly academic and impersonal, then my sample of producers.[1] They are all incredible people, and I am proud to introduce them to you here. They are presented in alphabetical order without any other categorization because they are all unique, and each one brings their own special something to independent film.

John Baldecchi	Toby Halbrooks	Peter Phok
Varda Bar-Kar	Andrew Harvey	Stu Pollard
Rob Barnum	Gill Holland	Stuart Pollok
Peter Billingsley	Carly Hugo	Doug Pray
Bill Borden	Jon Keeyes	Ross Putman
Todd Burns	Rosanne Korenberg	Diane Quon
Marc Butan	Greg Lauritano	Nick Raslan
Seth Caplan	Maximillian Leo	Matthew Rhodes
Milan Chakraborty	Dimitri Logothetis	Jeff Sackman
Chevy K. Chen	Cybill Lui	Joel Shapiro
Naomi Despres	Julie Lynn	James Short
Felipe Dieppa	Bill MacDonald	Nick Spicer
A.J. Dix	Thomas Mahoney	Nicholas Tabarrok
Scott Einbinder	Matt Manjourides	Jason Tamasco
Maurice Fadida	Tom McNulty	Andrew van den Houten
Eric Fleischman	Tim O'Hair	Scott Veltri
Ricky Fosheim	Siena Oberman	Chuck West
Lisa France	Matt Parker	Lisa Wolofsky
Mike Gabrawy	Alessandra Pasquino	Janet Yang
Cathy Gesualdo	Judd Payne	Brad Zions
Stephen Gibler	Clay Pecorin	
Zaheer Goodman-Bhyat	Josh Penn	
	Clark Peterson	

It is an impossible task to speak with all of the successful independent film producers around the world, as much as I would like to. For disclosure purposes, and for those of you who are statistically inclined, I made efforts to reduce bias in the sample, by making it large and diverse. There are men, women, people of color, people raised in many parts of the world, and people from a wide variety of educational and career backgrounds. Those interviewed included people I worked with, friends of friends, and people introduced to me by other producers, financiers, and other industry professionals.

When I share statistical insights throughout the book, I focus exclusively on the 50 U.S.-based producers who predominantly make narrative features. I exclude the documentary producers and those based outside of the United States from my statistics, because they are a little trickier to study financially. (Both of those groups use grants to fund their budgets, which is rarely a viable financial tool for domestic narrative producers, as I'll explain in Chapter 6.) The producers that are not included in the statistical analysis provided valuable anecdotes and advice that is shared throughout the book.

To give you a snapshot of the producers in my sample, I will share a few things I know about them. There is a wide range of experiences amongst the 50 producers. The first film that each raised money for was released sometime between 1986 and 2021, with the average in 2006. Many of these producers built the foundations for their careers when VHS and DVD were meaningful sources of revenue for a film, while others have only known a world dominated by streaming services.

There are lots of ways that the people performing the job of a producer are credited on a film. Often, they receive credit through a delicate set of negotiations as either a producer, executive producer, co-producer, or associate producer.[2] I also know of producers who only received credit as a director, writer, actor, and, in one case, "thanks." That said, the most desirable credit is producer, because it is a title that denotes power and prestige. The average subject in this sample received a producer credit on IMDB for 8.8 completed films by the time that they sat for their interview, but that number maxes out at 27 for one producer in the group. Both of those values would be much higher if executive producer credits were included in my count.

There are lots of ways to categorize career success, beyond just the number of films produced. Another way is to look at box office. Amongst my 50 producers, the average lifetime box office receipts are about $36 million. The average is pushed up substantially by three producers with more than $500 million of lifetime box office. Twenty-two subjects in the sample have a lifetime box office under $1 million. Keep in mind that many films skip a theatrical release, and go to another distribution platform initially, such as a streaming service or a cable network. Therefore, lifetime box office is a weak measure of career success.

Table 1.1 A Snapshot of the Producers' Careers

This table shows four different metrics that demonstrate the range of the 50 producers' careers. The minimum is the smallest or earliest value, and the maximum is the largest or latest number. The 1st Film is the first movie for which the producer successfully raised a substantial amount of the cash needed for production. Producer Credits counts the number of times the person is credited as "Producer" for a narrative feature film on IMDB. Lifetime Box Office is the sum of the box office on all of an individual's films with a Producer Credit, as reported by the-numbers.com. IMDB Votes is the sum of all votes for all of a person's films with a Producer Credit.			
Career Metric	Average	Minimum	Maximum
Year of 1st Film	2006	1986	2021
Producer Credits	9	4	27
Lifetime Box Office ($ millions)	35.9	0.0	511.0
IMDB Votes	100,022	217	475,597

One peculiar thing that I noticed is that producers are concerned with something *Stowaway* filmmaker Maximilian Leo called the Taxi Driver Test. Maybe you've heard of it? Imagine that a producer gets into a taxi in a random city, and then the conversation goes like this:

INT. TAXI IN A NONDESCRIPT BIG CITY - NIGHT

The driver is stunningly handsome, with remarkable charisma, suggesting he can do much bigger things in life.

                    DRIVER
                What do you do?

                    PASSENGER
                Well . . .

Passenger winces and squirms a bit, recognizing that the test is about to begin, yet again.
                  PASSENGER (cont'd)
            I'm a movie producer!

                    DRIVER
         Oh yeah? What'd you make?

                  PASSENGER
"Delta and Omicron," "The Butter and The Knife," "The Knob That Twists."

Choose your own ending! Does the Driver say:

```
            1) DRIVER
I love those! You're working on great stuff!

                 Or

            2) DRIVER
Huh, interesting, I've never seen them. I like
                Marvel.
```

Obviously, every independent producer prefers #1 over #2. In addition to considering the number of films produced and the lifetime box office, we can also measure the likelihood of the producer passing the Taxi Driver Test by counting how many votes their films have earned on IMDB.[3] Presumably, the more votes, the better the chances that the driver has seen the movie. The goal is to find out if people are watching their films and their work is having some measurable impact on the world, besides creating jobs on set.

The average producer in my sample has tallied 100,022 votes on IMDB for the films that they are credited as producer (not co-producer, executive producer, associate producer, etc.) The number of votes ranges from 217 at the low end to about 476,000. It is reasonable to believe that some producers I interviewed are more likely to pass the Taxi Driver Test than others.

My subjects are all at different points in their careers. Some are still in their mid-20s and just getting started, while others are preparing to slow down and enjoy the good life. Some of the differences in the IMDB vote totals amongst producers are due to the social impact of the films that they made – some movies are more beloved than others. However, some of it is also driven by how many films they made. I promise to explore that more in Chapter 13.

Despite the fact that only about one-sixth of the producers in the sample claim to be from the Greater Los Angeles, California metropolitan area (LA), 72% indicate that they are working in LA now.[4] Many producers supplement their income with jobs related to the movie business, such as teaching courses at film schools, directing television commercials, and providing consulting services. Therefore, working out of LA provides additional opportunities to earn an income and connect with other professionals. The other producers in the sample are mostly working out of New York, with a pocket of three in Kentucky, one in the San Francisco Bay area, one in Idaho, and one in Colorado.

Film school is the most common educational path for the subjects in this sample, representing 39% of the respondents. Law degrees and MBAs were also frequently-mentioned academic degrees, with each being earned by 8% of producers. At least two out of the 50 did not attend college.

Despite making an intentional effort to begin my interviews with women, men dominated the sample. Only 14% of the respondents are female. In almost every case that I asked a female producer to recommend another producer to be interviewed, she put forth the name of a male producer. I do not think that is due to any bias, but rather the current, male-dominated state of the business. For instance, only 25% of the producers receiving an Oscar nomination for Best Picture from 2010–2022 are female.

Subjects were not asked to report their ethnic or racial identity. As a casual observer, I would say that almost all are White or Caucasian, although about 10% are Asian. Only one producer that I interviewed referred to himself as Black. I would have preferred more racial diversity in the sample, but almost every time I was introduced to another producer, it was a White person. This lack of diversity mirrors the 2021 "Producers Sustainability Survey Report" sample from the "Dear Producer" blog.

In the pages that follow, I try my best to capture the financial wisdom of these producers. They will help tell the story of independent film finance, as they lived it. So let's go!

Notes

1 The word "sample" is a bit of statistics jargon, meaning I didn't interview every living producer, only these folks. It's kind of like saying I didn't eat the whole tub of ice cream, I just took a sample.
2 Many producers laughed when asked to differentiate between their producing credits, because the lines are blurry. Even the Producers Guild of America does not have a firm definition of a producer.
3 IMDB users may voluntarily submit a rating for a given film, on a scale of one to ten. IMDB calls each submitted rating a vote. I use IMDB because I think it has the most votes of any platform, and it reports the exact number of votes cast. For instance, for *Fight Club*, IMDB has 2,008,342 votes on the day I'm writing this, versus a reported "250,000+" for Rotten Tomatoes.
4 The top three places of origin are the New York City region (22%), LA (16% of producers), and Ohio (8%).

2 The (Movie) Business

> Understand the market and the ecosystem that you're a part of.
> – Marc Butan, producer

> If I wasn't in this business to make money, I'd do something useful with my life.
> – Jeff Sackman, producer

We all have a favorite awkward moment in history when art and commerce collided, right?

On October 5, 2018, a painting by the artist Banksy shredded itself inside Sotheby's auction house in London, seconds after a buyer paid $1.4 million for it. Needless to say, this was not what the buyer had in mind when they made the purchase. As a street artist, Banksy was attempting to mock the collector and the system that allowed them to grow their wealth. This is a beautiful intersection of art and business, where one tried to destroy itself to spite the other. (The collector got the last laugh, as the work became instantly famous, and sold for $25.4 million three years later.)

Movies are one of the greatest, most influential art forms ever created. Their ability to quickly bond audiences and influence opinions are amazing. Families get excited every year to watch classics like *A Christmas Story* together, while documentaries such as *Blackfish* and *An Inconvenient Truth* shift the mood of the public incredibly fast. The medium is tied to national morale, and it has endured wars, recessions, pandemics, and countless other tragedies. (I am sure you and I could sit around and talk for hours about why movies are socially invaluable.) Yet, all of these great films are businesses, created with a profit motive.

Movies are also the most expensive art form ever created, with the budgets of several Marvel titles reportedly exceeding $500 million.[1] I promise that Disney is not giving that money away just to create a vibrant community of artists like writers, costumers, set decorators, and visual effects animators. Disney fully expects to get paid back and earn a profit.

DOI: 10.4324/9781003363446-4

This is where we go from movies to the movie business.

In order to get your movie made, you will need to think of your movie as a business. It is a money-making venture. You will create a separate legal entity – using a limited liability corporation (LLC) or similar structure – that owns everything from the rights to your movie to the final cut. You will be one owner of that business, and there could be many others.

It will be your job to make sure that your film makes money. There are only two ways to do that: distribution and intellectual property (IP). This chapter gives you more details about how both avenues bring money to films.

Production Business

> It all has to come together in a perfect way at just the right time.
> – Lisa Wolofsky, producer

Your movie can only make money if it is finished. You will spend cash in production first. This section is all about the structure of the production business.

Major Studios

> The studio path can lead to never, or it can lead to many, many years before you get something made.
> – Brad Zions, producer

As I'm writing this, there are six major studios: Disney, Netflix, Paramount, Sony Pictures, Universal, and Warner Bros. There are two reasons that these are considered major studios.

First, they are the only members of the Motion Picture Association (MPA). The MPA is the organization that sets movie ratings in the United States. The MPA decides whether your movie is rated PG-13 or R. It also lobbies on behalf of its members for better tax incentives and more piracy protections. A studio cannot choose to join the MPA, but instead must be invited. Lionsgate was allegedly offered membership but refused (they didn't see the value in paying dues in excess of $20 million per year, according to *The Hollywood Reporter*). Amazon Studios is likely to join soon if they have not already.

Second, all six major studios have the means to distribute their films mostly on their own around the world. While Netflix has its service in 190 countries and Universal Pictures has subsidiaries throughout the largest economies, indie studio A24 only has distribution capabilities in the United States. When it releases a film like *Everything Everywhere All At Once*, it has to use a network of over 20 foreign distributors to get the movie to consumers.

With the exception of Netflix, the major studios primarily produce films for theaters. All buy Sony own a streaming service too. Disney+/Hulu, HBO Max (Warner Bros.), Netflix, Paramount+, and Peacock (Universal) are all streamers operated by the majors studios in the United States. In addition, they compete with AppleTV+, Amazon's Prime Video, and a number of smaller services for consumers' attention. Not all of them will last.

In business, industries typically mature to only support three dominant competitors. This concept is known as the "Rule of Three," and it works in so many different segments of the economy (such as phone service providers, fast food burger restaurants, and movie theater chains). Sometimes an industry will only support two dominant firms, and other times four, but it is usually three. We can expect streaming to consolidate in the same way. The seven major players in streaming in the United States will not all survive. There will be fewer in the years to come, and they will collectively produce fewer movies as a result.

Independent Studios

Independent studios are all of the other companies that produce films but are not major studios. People also use terms such as mini-major studio and production/distribution company to describe the larger independent production companies that exist in this space. What all of these companies have in common is that they have an existing pool of money and a permanent workforce within the company that is working to develop new films. I would include in this group everything from the biggest companies with distribution arms, like A24 and Neon, to the smaller, talent-focused production companies like Wes Anderson's Indian Paintbrush and Reese Witherspoon's Hello Sunshine.

There is a long line of mini-major studios that no longer exist. They struggle with longevity for one of three reasons. First, if they are successful and develop a nice library of films with valuable IP, then they are usually acquired by another firm. We saw this with Lionsgate's acquisition of *Twilight* producer Summit Entertainment, and Disney's 2009 purchase of Marvel Studios. Second, many overspend and fall into financial distress, recently including once-rising stars Annapurna Pictures, Global Road, and Relativity Media.

The third category of mini-major disappearances are those that just run out of money and wrap up operations neatly. Very often, smaller studios begin with a large pool of money from an investor that represents a one-time commitment. The producers running these operations are provided enough funding to develop and make a small slate of between six and ten movies. They can continue to make additional movies if they generate enough cash from the initial slate to fund them. That means they need to earn a big win in their first batch of movies to stay in business. These studios disappear when they burn through their cash and cannot find new investors. Once the money runs out, they sell their library and shut off the lights.

Independent Producers

> Indie filmmaking is more of a business than it ever was.
> – Matthew Parker, producer

That's you! And thousands of other people. Independent producers do everything from the inception of the idea (the fun stuff!) to the closing down of the business (the not fun stuff). Independent producers can work for independent studios, or can work for themselves. The movie business exists in large part because independent producers manufacture thousands of films each year, independent of the major studios, independent of influence on their ideas, and independent of efforts to control the output of production.

Think of all of the people who benefit from the tireless work of independent producers: movie theaters, streaming platforms, television channels, lenders, agents, managers, prop rental houses, and so many more.

Yet, independent producers are the most powerless people in the movie business. They have to beg investors for money. They have to beg authors for IP. They have to beg stars to appear in their films. They have to beg festivals to get a screening. They have to beg distributors to take their films for a decent price. They have to beg for media coverage. They are at the mercy of guilds, sound stage owners, and the ratings agencies around the world. Arguably, independent producers lack power over any part of the movie business because of their independence. The economics of independent production are challenging, and go a long way to explain why it is so hard to be an independent producer.

Economic power always rests in the hands of the party with access to the most scarce of resources. Throughout history, families have grown wealthy with their access to salt, gold, oil, railroads, and other assets that had to be rationed. Today, new wealth is being grown by people with access to a different breed of scarce resources: space (Elon Musk), our very personal data (Mark Zuckerberg), and our limited time for shopping (Jeff Bezos).

Independent producers inherently work in the opposite direction, away from scarcity. *Hotel Mumbai* producer Mike Gabrawy, using terrific economic jargon, says that "there are no barriers to entry in independent film." Anyone can be a producer, and so many people try. As a result, there is a new flood of independent films on the market each year. There are so many equity-financed independent films with little or no value.

The economics of independent production cannot change for the better. Despite the calls for change, it will always be difficult to sustain a career making independent films. There will always be hungry, young producers hustling to make their movies, and working in the opposite direction from scarcity. The nature of being an independent producer will always be one of chasing the scarce resources, and producer Peter Phok would tell you, "you aren't entitled to any of it."

I know these few paragraphs on the economics of independent production are less rosy than you or I would like. Let me help you step back and remember that there are thousands of people making a living as an independent producer. What they all have in common is the ability to look past the negativity and get the job done. If you can do that too, right now, in this moment, then there is real hope for you as an independent producer.

I shared this information so that you will understand the economic environment and a few of the challenges that lie ahead. I do not mean to say that all independent producers are starving. While movies are not scarce, great movies with the potential to be huge hits are uncommon – and this is a hits-driven business. The producers who can consistently make that type of film are scarce, and they are paid well. Stars chase them, studios chase them, and investors chase them. May that be you someday!

Talent Agencies

> If you have a great relationship with a certain agent, then they're going to feed you their clients and help you get it financed.
> – Matthew Parker, producer

It is hard to talk about the business of production without mentioning the vital role of the talent agencies.[2] Talent agents primarily exist to get their clients roles on shows (by which I mean films, episodic programs, and any other filmed content that will pay them). It is the agent's job to know which upcoming parts might be a good fit for their client, and then convince the decision-makers to hire and pay the client well, with the agent getting a 10% commission on all compensation. On their own, a talent agent representing a few clients is not very impactful to the business. However, an army of agents with a roster of attractive clients together is a powerful organization.

One of the biggest talent agencies, Creative Artists Agency (CAA), is famously known for their unique structure where their clients are represented by the entire agency, and not just one agent. In fact, former agent Jessica Tuchinsky discloses in "The Movie Business Book," that "an agent can only sign a new client with the consent of the entire department" (pg. 218). This type of collaboration makes CAA and its peers very powerful parts of the Hollywood machinery.

One way that the agencies wield their power is by packaging their clients together – a screenwriter, a director, and a few actors – to make a movie. As a producer, packaging can work for you or against you. If the agency is gathering talent around your film, then that makes your life much easier. However, if they are packaging their stars on other producers' projects, then that makes it harder for you to get access to the talent you need on yours.

The talent agencies are also hubs of information. It is their job to know everybody – all of the people and businesses supporting the creation of new shows, from major studios down to small producers – and not just actors, writers, and directors. Plus, they are connected to attorneys, financiers and distributors. On top of that, they know the scripts that are floating around, who is lined up to be in which role, and how much they will be paid. These days, talent agencies are also involved in financing and selling movies. They use those arms of their businesses to feed even more information into their machinery. There is no doubt that the talent agencies have a huge informational advantage over independent producers, which gives them more power and control.

Most importantly, talent agencies are the gate keepers of your on-screen stars. Matthew Parker will tell you that "the people with the best relationships (with the talent agencies) do better." Marc Butan, producer of *Killing Them Softly*, said, "I find agencies to be quite helpful if you know what you're asking them to do."

Only work experience allows you to build relationships and understand the talent agencies' business, so you know what you're asking them to do. Several of the producers interviewed for this book began their careers at agencies. They learned the inner workings and built connections through those jobs. That is why Charlize Theron's producing partner A.J. Dix encourages young filmmakers to "get into a talent agency." Others started at production companies where they had meaningful interactions with talent agencies and learned how to navigate the business from the outside. Felipe Dieppa got to know agents, their business, and "the language to use" as a child actor, lending his voice to Diego in *Dora the Explorer*. He learned that, "they're just people – it's pretty easy to call and ask if they're interested." One way or another, understanding the talent agencies and maintaining strong relationships with the people on the inside are key skills in the producer's toolbox.

Distribution

> If you can't get your movie distributed, then your movie doesn't exist.
> – John Baldecchi, producer

On December 26, 1906, the world's first feature film, *The Story of the Kelly Gang*, opened at the Athenaeum Theatre in Melbourne, Australia. In bold letters at the bottom of the ads announcing its release, the producers added the financially relevant phrase, "POPULAR PRICES!" Over 100 years ago, the only way to monetize a movie was by showing it to lots of ticket-buying people in giant theaters.

Over time, many other means have emerged for people to watch a movie. In the 1950s, viewers began to see films like *The Wizard of Oz* on network television on a Saturday or Sunday night. HBO launched in 1972, and suddenly cable TV gave households the chance to pay for channels showing movies without commercials. Then home video – Betamax (1975), VHS (1976), DVD (1996), Blu-Ray (2006), and digital download (2008) – allowed families to rent or own a copy. Now, premium and ad-supported streaming services provide new platforms for watching everything from familiar classics to new releases.[3]

All of these ways of watching a movie are known as windows, and each window provides another opportunity for your film to make money. Windows are a great business design, and they still exist to some extent for most films. They allow the people who are the most excited to see the movie – the superfans—to pay the most. These are the consumers who will buy the expensive tickets on the opening Friday night, in the theater, on an IMAX screen. For more patient consumers, the film might be available at matinee pricing the following Tuesday. If they were willing to wait a few months, they could rent it from iTunes or Redbox at a much lower price. For those who did not mind waiting a little longer, it would be included in their Netflix or pay TV subscription price. Five years later, it might be free on cable channel 3456 with 22 minutes of REALLY LOUD ads per hour.

This process, of making the most money from those who are willing to pay the most, is known by economists as price discrimination. It works with movies, it works with sports (the closer to the field, the more you pay), and it works with airlines (the more comfortable you want to be on the plane, the more you pay). Price discrimination has been the machine that made independent film work for many years, and explains why so many people want a theatrical release for their project.

To make price discrimination function, your film needs distributors around the world. If your movie is following a traditional windowing strategy, the task of the distributor is to get your movie into local theaters, and then sell it to TV channels and streaming services in their market, and maybe sell physical media (DVDs and Blu-rays) into stores.[4] Depending on your agreement, they may also advertise your film for you.

In proper industry lingo, your distributor sells your film to exhibitors. Typically, the term exhibitor is associated with movie theaters. However, any business that shows the finished film to customers is an exhibitor, whether that is a movie theater, or a non-theatrical exhibitor, like an airline or local television channel. Note that some streaming services can be a producer, distributor, and an exhibitor all in one. For example, Netflix makes a movie, and then they distribute it globally on their own platform, where subscribers watch it.

To do all of this work for your film, the distributor charges a fee, based on the money that your film generates. Typically, they will take about 40¢ out of every dollar. They will also require all of their expenses to be repaid by the money generated by the movie before they begin paying you. For instance, if they buy local TV ads for your film, the distributor gets repaid for the cost of those commercials before you get repaid.

Please, PLEASE, be very careful to pick a reputable distributor. The world is full of producers who handed rights to a shady distributor, and then never saw a penny for their work. Do lots of homework before signing a contract. It is very easy to get trapped into a contract that locks up your movie for ten years and pays you nothing. Ask other producers about their experiences with specific distributors. The ones who have been burned will gladly tell you the whole, gory story. A great resource to learn more about the pitfalls of distribution is Alex Ferrari's podcast, "Indie Film Hustle." As I always tell new producers, please get a good entertainment attorney who knows independent film distribution contracts well.

Let me also add that you could distribute your film yourself, but chances are you will not. Very few producers self-distribute, and I've never heard a story about someone's life-changing success distributing their own film. Distribution is a full-time job that requires a specialized skill set and the right connections. Most producers choose to allocate their time to producing, and leave distribution to someone who enjoys it.

Ultimately, you want your movie seen by audiences around the world. You can't show it to everyone yourself, so you need distributors to get your project onto DVDs in Croatia, and cable TV in Turkey, and the fourth largest streaming service in Nigeria. Distributors get your film to consumers in every window, from theatrical to free TV, and generate money that can be used to repay your investors. To find the distributors who will give you the most money for your film, you are probably going to hire a sales agent. For instance, *Nice Guys*, starring Russell Crowe and Ryan Gosling, had over 20 international distributors. According to the *Hollywood Reporter*,[5] they were:

Australia and New Zealand (Roadshow), Benelux (Belga), Eastern Europe Block (Freeman), France (EuropaCorp), Germany (TMG), Greece (Odeon), Hong Kong (PT Parkit), Indonesia (PT Amero), Israel (United King), Italy (Lucky Red), Latin America (SUN), Malaysia (PT Parkit), Philippines (PT Parkit), Scandinavia (Mislabel), Singapore (Golden Village), South Africa (Times Media), South Korea (Scene & Sound), Spain (TriPictures), Switzerland (Ascot Elite), Taiwan (PT Parkit), Thailand (PT Parkit), Turkey/ME/India-Pakistan (Italia), U.K. (Icon), and Vietnam (PT Parkit).

Warner Bros. also had distribution rights in the United States.

The producers of *Nice Guys* did not find all of these distributors on their own. They hired a sales agency, Bloom, to do the work for them. The job of a sales agent is to find lots of good distributors around the world who want to, well, distribute your film. A sales agent knows all of the distributors, and works between them to get the best distribution deals for your film. Sales agents are your friends. They want your movie to sell, and they want to collect their 12%-ish fee off of all the revenue that your movie generates.

In the perfect world, first you will hire an entertainment attorney, then you will hire a sales agent, and then you will sign contracts with distributors, all before your movie becomes a global phenomenon.

All of these people come together at film markets and festivals, like Cannes, the American Film Market (AFM), Toronto International Film Festival (TIFF), and European Film Market (EFM) in Berlin. If you can make your way to one of these events in person, it's a great place to meet a lot of people and build a healthy network of professional connections in a very short time. (Former AFM Director Jonathon Wolf does lots of interviews about how to make the most of your time at the market. Find one that is current because AFM is evolving so rapidly.)

Ricky Fosheim, producer of *The Head Hunter*, will tell you that "you have to sell a movie many times." To achieve its full economic potential, your movie typically has to be sold to four different groups of buyers. First, you need to pitch (sell) your movie to a sales agent. You and your sales agent will then sell your movie to distributors. The distributors will sell it to exhibitors, including theater owners, streaming services, and TV channels. Finally, the exhibitors will sell it to consumers.

* * *

Just for fun, imagine that your movie earns $1 million at the box office. You're in the money! Or are you?

First, the government takes sales taxes. In the United States, that would be about 4% of the box office, but tax rates vary a lot around the world (approaching 50% in some parts of India). Your $1 million of U.S. box office receipts quickly becomes $960,000 after taxes. Then, the theater owner (exhibitor) gets to keep about half of that to pay for power-reclining seats, rent, and angst-filled teenagers to staff the joint, so your $960,000 becomes $480,000.

Next comes your distributor. If they spent $280,000 on social media and billboard ads, they get repaid for those before splitting the money with you. Of the $480,000, the remaining pie to be shared is only $200,000. Finally, your distributor gets paid 40% of that for doing their job, which comes out to $80,000. Of that inspiring $1 million of box office, there is only $120,000 left over.

The proceeds of $120,000 will hopefully go to your collection account manager (we'll talk more about them in Chapter 11). They do great work, but might take 1% for their troubles. With that haircut, you are down to $118,800.

Oh, and there's one other team that gets some of that box office revenue too. Your sales agent will charge you at least 10% of your revenues as a fee for doing their job. That leaves your film with just $106,920 from the original $1 million to repay your investors and compensate your talent.

Hopefully, this $106,920 is just from the United States, and there are lots of other distributors globally who are having similar success selling your movie to theater-goers. Add them all up, and you might do very well financially. (We will dig much more into the numbers in the following chapters.)

In summary, distribution is how your movie makes money. Distribution is where the art becomes a business. You need distribution to reach an audience, make an impact, reward your investors, and build a career.

In my courses at Loyola Marymount campus, I use the book *The Business of Media Distribution* by Jeffrey Ulin, to help my students understand how shows are monetized. Mr. Ulin does a great job at explaining all of the ways your film can make money, and I strongly recommend it as a resource.

Intellectual Property (IP)

Again, there are two ways to make money off your film, via distribution and through exploitation of the Intellectual Property (IP). IP is anything that is uniquely created for your film, and your film itself.

IP is all around you. As I write this book, I am sitting in a room that has a Shrek pinball machine, my kids' lightsabers, and a copy of the book *Fleabag: The Scriptures*. Congrats to DreamWorks Animation, LucasFilm, and Phoebe Waller-Bridge for successfully monetizing your IP!

All of these examples constitute different forms of IP. The pinball machine is Shrek-green, and adorned with characters and scenes from the movie. At one point in the game, Eddie Murphy, as Donkey, even says, "In the morning, I'm making waffles!" The pinball machine manufacturer was only able to use those characters, scenes, and audio recordings because they paid DreamWorks Animation for the right to do so. Similarly, a toy manufacturer paid LucasFilm for the right to recreate a prop, and a book publisher paid Phoebe Waller-Bridge for the right to print and bind her scripts from the ground-breaking television series *Fleabag*.

The reality is, you need successful distribution to have any hope of monetizing the IP. If your film succeeds in distribution, then fans are going to want more ways to connect with it. In the best-case scenario, your film is like *Star Wars*, where the props, spaceships, characters, and quotes from the script are all iconic, and all can be sold in one form or another for millions of dollars over many years.

A more reasonable expectation is that you might get to make sequels or a TV series based on your successful film. The nice thing about sequels and TV series is that they provide you with a few years of career stability, and maybe a little more financial success. At the extreme end is the 2019 film *Knives Out*, produced independently by Rian Johnson and Ram Bergman, and distributed by Lionsgate. It made $311 million worldwide at the box office, with a reported budget of just $40 million. With that kind of public reception, Bergman and Johnson shopped the sequels around to other distributors to find the best deal. In the end, Netflix agreed to pay $469 million for the next two films. (Bergman and Johnson do not get to keep all $469 million, because they have to use some of it to fund the sequels.)

Star Wars and *Knives Out* are outliers that show the potential to monetize your film's IP, both through consumer products and sequels. The reality is that most independent films do not get to monetize their IP beyond the film's release, but the possibility is there.

Takeaways

- There are many companies in the movie business, and they all exist to make money.
- Your movie will be monetized through its distribution and the exploitation of the IP.

Notes

1 Joe Russo, the director of *Avengers: Infinity War* and *Avengers: Endgame*, told an audience at the Sands International Film Festival of St. Andrews (Scotland) in 2022 that "each of those movies was $500 million plus."

2 It is such a vital part of the business that states including California, Florida, New Jersey, and New York have a series of laws regulating talent agents. See: https://www.agentassociation.com/index.php?src=directory&view=agencyLicensing&srctype=detail&back=agencyLicensing&refno=38
3 I acknowledge that piracy exists as a way to watch a movie. I do not include it here because it doesn't make money for the producer.
4 The DVD business has been stubbornly persistent, with nearly $2 billion of physical media sold just in the United States in 2021. In comparison, $16.3 billion was sold at the peak in 2005, according to the Digital Entertainment Group. DVD revenue will disappear eventually, but it will take many more years to fade to black.
5 See: https://www.hollywoodreporter.com/movies/movie-news/afm-russell-crowe-ryan-goslings-747529/

3 The Language of Business

> It's just a business. You have to sell it for more than it costs.
> – Jeff Sackman, producer

I want to forewarn you that there is a lot of finance jargon in this chapter, and I encourage you to reread it a few times to make sure you understand it all. (Humans learn best through repetition. And did you know that humans learn best through repetition?)

BUT do not skip ahead to the next chapter, because this is really important!

The words that I use are the same that your potential investor will use. If you do not understand them, I promise that you will not get their money to make your film. This chapter teaches you the language of business.

In all university business programs around the world, an accounting course is required, even though many students find the subject to be dull and tedious. The accounting courses are always required because accounting is the language of business. Let me show you what I mean, starting with this headline from CNN on August 5, 2021:

> 'South Park' creators score reported $900 million deal with ViacomCBS

Can you tell from that headline whether the creators, Trey Parker and Matt Stone, get to keep all $900 million or if they are required to spend part of it? To answer that question, let me show you a very simple income statement:

$$\begin{array}{r} \text{Revenues} \\ \underline{-\text{ Costs}} \\ \text{Profits} \end{array}$$

Every business has an income statement. Every movie has an income statement. Even you have a personal income statement (wages – rent/utilities/food/concert tickets/etc. = savings). *South Park* does too. Income statements are always structured like this, with costs subtracted from revenues to find profits. Revenues are the money coming into the business from the sale of its good or services. Costs are generally all of the things that the company has to spend money on to keep the business running. The income statement is one of the two fundamental financial statements that you need in order to understand what is happening with your film.

In this case, ViacomCBS (later renamed Paramount Global) is providing Parker and Stone $900 million of revenue. The $900 million goes on the top line of the income statement, not the bottom line. The important implication is that the *South Park* creators don't get to keep it all. They are required to spend much of it making episodes and movies, which Paramount gets to distribute. Parker and Stone's profits will be the difference between the revenues and the costs they eventually incur producing those shows. (Notice, there are those words again: revenues, costs, and profits.) They and their advisors presumably estimated their costs, and then agreed to a revenue number that ensures that the profits are much bigger than $0. In other words, they should not lose money on this arrangement.

Parker and Stone are also doing something here that all veteran producers try to accomplish: they are generating the cash needed to make the shows by selling them first, before they ever exist. This is backwards from how most businesses run. If you want to run a lemonade stand, you first need to buy a pitcher, some lemons, sugar, cups, and posterboard for signs. Once the stand is set up and the lemonade is made, then you start selling it. In the language of business, your lemonade stand incurs its costs before you receive revenue. The *South Park* team did the opposite – they generated revenue before incurring costs. They were able to do so because their IP is valuable in the eyes of Paramount. (We'll talk more about generating cash in later chapters.)

Almost all of the producers that I interviewed incurred the costs of making their first movie before they received any revenue. If you just made a $250,000 movie, and have not received any revenue yet, then your income statement looks like this:

Revenue	$0
– Costs	$250,000
Profit	–$250,000

The bad news is that your profit is negative – you lost money, you're in the red. The good news is that you found $250,000 to spend in the first place! To explain where that $250,000 came from, we need another financial statement, the Balance Sheet.

There are three basic items on every balance sheet: assets, liabilities, and equity. Assets are the things that are valuable to the business, like cash, cameras, trucks, and IP. Assets have a monetary value, and are usually things that you can physically touch with your hand, but not always. For instance, someday soon, your most important asset will be the movie that you just made. You cannot touch your IP, because it is just a collection of ones and zeros stored in the cloud, but it has a monetary value.

The liabilities on the balance sheet are amounts that the business is required to pay in the future, like loans, deferred talent compensation, and credit card bills. There are two types of liabilities in the world: those that need to be paid with interest and those that do not. (If you don't know what interest is yet, don't worry. I promise we'll get there soon, because interest is the foundation of finance, the success of your movie, and your career.) For instance, when your talent defers $50,000 of compensation until the movie is released, you only ever have to pay $50,000. It does not matter whether the film is released in one year or five years. The amount paid is always the same with this type of liability because there is no interest. Liabilities that require money to be paid back in the future with interest, like credit cards, are called debts. All debts are liabilities, but not all liabilities are debts.

In addition to assets and liabilities, all business balance sheets have equity. Equity is the portion of the assets that belong to the owners of the firm (you!) after they pay their liabilities.

Assets, liabilities, and equity are always intimately tied together as follows:

$$Assets - Liabilities = Equity$$

$$- Or -$$

$$Assets = Liabilities + Equity$$

This is the most basic rule of accounting, and hopefully you can see that the two equations above say the exact same thing. The first version says that if you add up all of the stuff that you bought and made (assets) and then subtract out what you owe (liabilities), you are left with equity. The second version says that the money to pay for the assets has to come from either liabilities or equity.

The rule that Assets = Liabilities + Equity defines a balance sheet. A simple one looks like this:

Assets	Liabilities and Equity
Cash = $0	Liabilities = $0
Your Film = $250,000	Equity = $250,000
Total = $250,000	Total = $250,000

It is called a balance sheet because there are two sides, and they must be equal, or balance. One side is always your assets, which are the things that you own. In this case, you made a movie that you and your investors now own, and it is worth $250,000, but you spent all of your cash to make it. (It may be worth more once you sell it, but we do not know that yet.) On the other side are your investors – the people who gave you $250,000. In this example, your investors chose equity, not debt. The $250,000 of assets precisely balance with the $250,000 of equity. We have not broken any rules yet!

Between the income statement and the balance sheet, we can see the history of your film. First, the balance sheet says that you raised $250,000 of cash from equity investors. Then, the income statement shows that you incurred $250,000 in costs, which means that you spent all of your cash to make your movie. It also shows that you are waiting to receive revenue, so the balance sheet shows that your investors are still waiting to get their $250,000 back. I love financial statements because they tell stories like this, although they are almost always way more interesting than this simple example.

Now let's imagine that you sell your movie to a streaming service for $750,000. Your income statement changes to look like this:

Revenue	$750,000
– Costs	$250,000
Profit	$500,000

That's much better! Now you have a $500,000 profit, but we do not know yet whether you get to keep it. To figure that out, we need to see the new balance sheet first:

Assets	Liabilities and Equity
Cash^1 = $750,000	Liabilities = $0
Film = $0	Equity = $750,000
Total = $750,000	Total = $750,000

Notice that the value of your film went to $0, because you sold it off. In exchange, you got the $750,000 in cash. (You might still own the actual film, and it might or might not have value after its run on the streaming service ends.) In order to balance that $750,000 on the assets side, there needs to be $750,000 on the liabilities and equity side. Remember, the assets must always equal the combined value of the liabilities and equity. You do not owe any money, so the entire value flows through to the equity line. However, that still does not tell us how much of the $500,000 of profit you get to keep. To answer that question, we need to talk more about what equity is and how it works, and we will get there in a minute.

The important thing here is that you know the six key accounting terms that make the world go around: revenues, costs, profits, assets, liabilities, and equity. You will see all of these words throughout the rest of this book and throughout the rest of your career. If you are not quite comfortable with them yet, I encourage you to pause here and review this section. Remember, repetition is the key to learning.

Equi-wha-what? What Is Equity?

Matt Levine writes about finance for Bloomberg in really elegant, simple terms that make finance professionals jealous. My very favorite thing he ever wrote is this:

> The essence of finance is time travel. Saving is about moving resources from the present into the future; financing is about moving resources from the future back into the present.

Time travel! I love it! You and the investors in your movie are time travelers.

The reason that money needs to travel through time is shown on the income statements and balance sheets in the previous section. You need to spend the money to make your movie before you can sell it and generate revenue. In Matt Levine's terms, you need to move resources from the future back into the present. The cash generated by the sales of your film needs to be moved into the present so that you can spend it to make the movie. The way you get your revenue to time travel is by finding an investor who is willing to wait to spend their money in the future.

The key word that makes this arrangement work is "saving." In our modern economy, if your investor wants to save her money instead of spending it today, there are lots of institutions that will hold onto it for her, such as banks, mutual funds, and the government. In exchange for holding her money, these institutions will pay her a little extra cash each month, which is called interest. This interest is like free money, and its job is to incentivize your investor not to spend her money just yet. By saving her money rather than spending it, your investor gets more money.

It turns out that there are lots and lots of ways for your investor to save, and they all offer different amounts of interest. Generally, the safer ones offer less interest and the riskier ones offer more interest. We can call all of these savings options by one simple word: investments.

An investment that pays interest is said to provide a return, or a rate of return. Your potential investor may talk about interest, the return, the rate of return, the vig, or the premium she'll earn on her investment, and they all mean the same thing. She is not intentionally using different terms for interest to confuse you. The problem is that finance professionals have developed lots of different terms for interest. Just like there are 46 Icelandic words for snow, I teach at least 30 synonyms for interest in my introductory finance courses. All of these terms for interest just mean that someone is supposed to get back more money than they paid in.

One of the most common types of investments where people stash their savings is stock. When an investor buys stock, they are actually buying a small bit of equity in the company. For instance, Netflix's balance sheet on December 31, 2009 looked like this:

Assets	Liabilities and Equity
Assets = $902 million	Liabilities = $481 million
	Equity = $421 million
Total = $902 million	Total = $902 million

On that date, thousands of investors owned stock in Netflix. Some investors owned a lot, some owned very little. To give different amounts of equity to different investors, the stock is cut into shares. Netflix had 53,440,073 shares of stock that it had sold to investors on December 31, 2009. Each share of stock was worth $7.87, so a person with just one share owned 1/53,440,073rd of Netflix's equity.[2]

Just to recap, *equity* in big companies is made up of *stock*, and that stock is cut into *shares*, so some investors can own more and some can own less, depending on how much cash they have to save.

More importantly, all of those investors were expecting to earn interest on their Netflix stock. Netflix did not actually pay them interest, but if the price of the stock went up above $7.87, then the increase in the stock price would be just like a bank paying them interest. For instance, if you put $7.87 into a savings account at a bank, and earn 1.65% interest, then you will have $8.00. Similarly, if Netflix stock goes up 1.65%, then you can sell your share for $8.00. Either way, if your $7.87 turns into $8.00, you earned 1.65% interest. (Over the next decade, Netflix stock went up 4011%, to $323.57 per share, but that is another story for another day.)

Let me stress that Netflix never had to pay any interest to the owners of its stock. Equity investors are actually owners of the company. That investor with one share actually owns 1/53,440,073rd of Netflix! However, that ownership stake does not entitle the shareholder to very much. They can't walk into Netflix's office and take a chair. They don't get one minute of *Stranger Things* all to themselves. The owners are only legally entitled to whatever is left after all of the liabilities are paid.

Equity investors only get paid in one of three cases: 1) the company decides to pay some profits out as cash to its stockholders, which is called a dividend, 2) the company is acquired by another company, and all of the stock is bought with cash, or 3) the company sells off all of its assets (maybe in bankruptcy) and pays any remaining cash out to its shareholders. Companies pay dividends all the time, but my favorite is Microsoft's decision to pay out $32 billion in excess cash in 2004. It was such a big dividend that the United States government's Bureau of Economic Analysis issued a report on all of the ways it would skew their reported economic indicators. Companies are also acquired all the time resulting in payouts to equity investors, like Disney buying Fox. It is extremely rare for a company to sell off its remaining assets and distribute the cash to shareholders.

In easier terms, the equity investors get paid last. If you look at the right-hand side of the balance sheet, it is arranged from who gets paid first to who gets paid last when revenue arrives in the company's bank account. In proper legal jargon, an investor who is higher up on the balance sheet is said to have *priority* over an investor who is lower down. Lenders have priority over equity investors. Certain lenders even have priority over other lenders. For instance, in Netflix's case, they have some loans (these are called senior notes) and they have some credit cards (they call these unsecured revolving credit facilities). If they are running out of money, the loans get paid before the credit cards, and the equity investors get $0.

Some people call the right-hand side balance sheet the waterfall. You may also hear it called the capital structure and the financing stack – all mean the same thing. I will refer to it as the waterfall in this book, because that is the most common jargon used in the movie industry. People talk about the waterfall a lot, especially in regards to their position in the waterfall. My guess is that most do not know they are actually talking about the balance sheet. It can be our little secret. Once we get through a few more formalities, I will show you a sample waterfall for a movie in Chapter 11.

With all that backstory, we can now bring this all back to your film. When you ask a potential investor to put money into your movie, you are putting yourself in competition with all of the other ways that they could save their money. They could invest in you, but they could also invest in Disney stock, or Netflix stock, or a DeLorean, or a ranch in Montana, or countless other investments. You will need to convince them that they could get the most value out of choosing you over all other filmmakers and all other possible investments. This helps explain why it is so hard to find equity investors for independent films. Yet, there is so much more complexity to their choice than that.

Investors also know that the amount of interest that they are supposed to be paid is connected to the amount of risk that is inherent in the investment. Riskier investments must offer the possibility of a higher return to attract investors. Safer investments do not need to provide as much interest. This is known as the Risk-Return Tradeoff.

Think back to those investors who earned 4011% interest on their Netflix stock, instead of earning 1.65% interest in a bank savings account. The risk-return tradeoff explains the huge difference. A bank account is very safe, because the federal government will always give you back your money, even if the bank goes out of business. As a result, there is virtually no risk in saving at a bank. Netflix in 2009 was the polar opposite. They still did not have a well-established streaming service, while Blockbuster Video and Redbox were trying to steal their DVD-by-mail business. Netflix was just a couple of strategic mistakes away from going bankrupt, but also a couple of strategic choices away from being the company that we know today, so there was massive risk in buying their stock. If the potential return on Netflix stock was only 1.65%, then no investor would ever buy it, because they could get the same return with zero risk at the bank. Savers would only buy Netflix stock if they were compensated for taking on the massive risk, with a potential return much greater than 1.65%. The stockholders in this case recognized the large potential upside and decided to take the risk.

This massive disparity in interest rates is rare, but expected throughout finance, because of the immense difference in risk between the bank account and the Netflix stock. The risk-return tradeoff exists because investors demand more interest on riskier investments to be compensated for the possibility that they will lose some or all of their savings.

Risk is one of the keys of finance, and interconnected with our notion of time travel. Many equity investors put money into independent films, and are never repaid at all. A lot of money is lost when projects stall in development. Sometimes films are shot, but the producers run out of money before they complete the postproduction phase. Other films are finished, and never find distribution. If a film never generates revenue (top line on the income statement), then it can never produce profits (the bottom line) to repay its investors. There are lots of ways that the investor can lose their money, which means that there is a ton of risk in independent film investments.

The investor who gives you $250,000 today does not know when they will get their money back in the future (or even if they will get their money back), and how much interest they will be paid. All of those outcomes are determined by the amount of revenue that your film brings in down the road, and nobody knows that amount with certainty before it starts shooting. You need to compensate them for investing their money in your risky movie.

Do not despair my friend. All of this is to say that your investor expects their money back with a lot of interest. Independent films do find investors every day, and there are folks willing to take the risks, because producers figured out how to work with the risk-return tradeoff. Investors higher up in the waterfall, like banks, earn less interest, because getting paid first is the least-risky position. Equity investors, at the bottom of the waterfall, have the potential to earn much more interest, because they are in the riskiest position of being paid last. Independent film investors also get nonmonetary returns, such as going to the red carpet premiere, which still count in the risk-return tradeoff for some investors. You are empowered to structure your deals with investors so that they can earn a return that is appropriate for the amount of risk that they are shouldering. We will talk more about that later in this chapter.

Attracting investors to your film is possible. You just need to give them the right set of returns to put their money in your project.

Equity vs. Liabilities: Own vs. Owe

If you peek back at that Netflix balance sheet, you will notice that they had liabilities of $481 million and equity of $421 million. It is important that you understand the difference between liabilities and equity, and how they affect your movie.

In the classroom, I like to explain the difference with two words: own and owe. An equity investor is someone who owns part of the movie, just like you. They get to own their share forever, and keep collecting their slice of the profits as long as your movie is still generating revenue. The only way that an equity investor would be removed from the balance sheet is if they were paid a lot of money to buy their share of the business.

In contrast to equity, a liability means that you owe money to someone. This will typically be a bank or other lender, and they will always require you to repay what you owe, sometimes with interest. The great thing about liabilities is that they go away once you pay off what you owe, so they don't last forever like equity.

So there you have it: the difference between liabilities and equity is that you owe a debt but you own the equity. The much trickier part of liabilities and equity is figuring out which to use to finance your film.

Equity in Independent Film: The 120 and 50

The way equity has been defined so far, as the difference between assets and liabilities, is the way that virtually everyone in the world thinks about equity. Your new-to-the-business investors probably think of equity that way too. Of course, independent film bounces to the beat of its own drum, and defines *equity* a bit differently. It is really important that you understand both definitions, so that you can carry intelligent conversations with people inside and outside of the film business. For clarity, I will italicize *equity* in this section only when using the independent film definition.

Equity in independent film is not just traditional equity or traditional debt, but both. I will show you that an *equity* investment position typically consists of both a loan to be repaid with a premium and a share of the profits.

A unique structure has evolved to repay *equity* investors, called "The 120 and 50." To see how this structure works, imagine your aunt gives you $100 to start a lemonade stand. The '120' part means that she wants $120 back on her $100 investment. The '50' part means that she also wants 50% of your profits, after you pay her the $120. The balance sheet for your lemonade stand once she makes the investment would be as follows:

Assets	Liabilities and Equity
Cash = $100	Liabilities = $120
	Equity:
	Your Aunt = – $10
	You = – $10
Total = $100	Total = $100

The equity positions would both have to be negative to make the balance sheet balance. If the business turns out successful, the signs will flip to positive. To make that work, let's imagine your lemonade stand is a wild success! The income statement is as follows:

Revenue	$300
– Costs	$80
Profit	$220

From this success, all of the profits would go into the cash side of the balance sheet. It changes as follows:

Assets	Liabilities and Equity
Cash = $220	Liabilities = $120
	Equity:
	Your Aunt = $50
	You = $50
Total = $220	Total = $220

First, you are required to repay your aunt $120, so your cash goes from $220 to $100 ($220 – $120 = $100). Then you need to share half of the remaining $100 with her, so she gets $50 and you end up with $50. In total, your aunt receives $170 ($120 + $50 = $170). She invested $100 initially, so she gains $70 of interest.

Your film is not that different from this lemonade stand, financially speaking. The 120 and 50 in independent film pays your *equity* investors back similarly. They will recoup their initial investment plus 20% interest. Some people call the 20% interest a "20% premium" or a "20% vig," but they all mean the same thing. Generally, the 20% is completely independent of time. It does not matter whether your movie makes enough money to repay the 20% this year or in 15 years. You will pay the exact same dollar amount – 20% of the initial investment – whenever the cash is available.

This 120 piece of the 120 and 50 structure is actually a debt, because it is contractually required to be paid with interest. Once the *equity* investors get their 120, then they get 50% of all future profits from the film. As a result, *equity* in independent film is really a combination of debt and equity. An *equity* investor is both a lender and an equity holder.

There is a strong possibility that you will have more than one *equity* investor, and they will need to share the 50% of future profits. Typically, that piece of the pie is rationed out based on how much everyone invested. For instance, if two aunts both contributed $50 to your lemonade stand instead of one aunt contributing $100, then they would share equally in the $50 of profits allocated for *equity* investors. Each aunt would get $25 of those profits. They would each still get back their $50 investment plus a 20% premium too, which would pay them an additional $60. In total, they would then receive $60 + $25 = $85, or half of what your one aunt received in the original example.

Every producer that I asked about the 120 and 50 use terms like "the industry standard" to describe it. Ironically, they also told me that neither 120 nor 50 is set in stone. You and your investor will negotiate over the exact numbers and priorities. For instance, some producers convinced their investors to agree on 105 instead of 120, while others had to take 150 because they had no other options in a time of crisis. Similarly, producers noted some wiggle room around the 50% value. It is best to think of the 120 and 50 as a starting point for your negotiations, and not a given.

Although complicated, the 120 and 50 evolved to solve two concerns. First, *equity* investors understand that independent films are ridiculously risky, and getting back some of their money earlier helps reduce the risk. As you will see in the waterfall in Chapter 11, the 120 is always paid back ahead of some of the other claims on the film's profits. The 120 is higher priority. Second, *equity* investors want to collect big time if the film is a hit. The 50 gives them a sizable share of the profits after all of the liabilities are paid. As much as it is complicated, the 120 and 50 is an elegant design to manage the risk-return tradeoff and incentivize *equity* investments.

The key takeaway is that the 120 and 50 gives your *equity* investor a comfortable amount of interest if your film does moderately well, and a lot of interest if your film is a big hit. It compensates them for taking a huge risk by investing in you. And it will definitely be part of your negotiations with your potential *equity* investors.

Equity in the Real World

> You build momentum over time. The more people you meet, the more festivals you go to, the more films you make, the more you're going to meet the companies that are set up specifically to finance films.
> – Ross Putman, producer & agent

Given that I interviewed 50 narrative feature producers for this book, I can give you some data on how they used *equity* early in their career. About 86% of the money raised to finance their first narrative feature came from *equity* investments. That is also true if we just focus on the half of producers who started their careers before 2006 or those who started after. In order to get your first feature made, you almost definitely need to be successful at courting *equity* investors or bring on a producer who can do that work for you.

As you gain more success in your career, you might become less reliant on *equity*. While 86% of the money came from *equity* on first films, it is down to 70% on second films. More parts of the film finance ecosystem open up for producers once they gain some wins.

The *equity* can come from one of three sources: personal networks (themselves, or their friends and family), high-net-worth individuals, or institutions (studios, production companies, and financial firms). On first films, the *equity* predominantly comes from personal networks 37% of the time, while high-net-worth individuals lead the investment on 53%. Only 10% of first films are primarily financed by institutions.

The budgets on these films are markedly different too. First films with the *equity* from the producers' personal networks had an average budget of $360,000. If the *equity* mostly came from high-net-worth individuals, then the average budget was $2.2 million. Institutionally funded first-films typically spent $2.7 million. These results make it pretty clear that raising money from high-net-worth individuals beyond your personal network should be your goal, unless you have that legendary rich uncle in your family.

I do not have the data to prove it, but I suspect that the reason that more first films are made with *equity* from high-net-worth individuals instead of personal networks is that it is really hard to get enough cash from your friends and family to make a quality production. You probably have to get to know people beyond your inner circle in order to get your movie made, and we will talk more about how to find those people in Chapter 14.

The producers who do not use their personal networks to finance their first film arguably have more successful careers. There are two ways to measure career success that I use throughout this book. The first is with box office, measured as the total worldwide revenue that the producer's films earn at the box office, as reported by Bruce Nash's the-numbers.com. The second way to measure career success is motivated by Maximilian Leo's taxi driver test in Chapter 1. To estimate the likelihood of a random taxi driver seeing the movie, I count the total number of votes for each film on IMDB. Presumably, the more votes, the more people who have seen it.

My statistics show that the producers who gain *equity* investments from high-net-worth individuals on their first films have not earned significantly more at the box office over their careers that those whose *equity* investors are within their personal networks. However, the producers who get institutional *equity* investments have earned $43 million more in lifetime box office.³

The statistics on IMDB votes are clearer. A producer who is able to find a high-net-worth investor for their first film has 74,000 more votes on average than a producer who relied on their personal network. The gap is even larger for the producers who found institutional investors, gaining 105,000 more votes.

Collectively, all of this evidence suggests that it is possible to build a successful career even if you raise the *equity* for your first feature from your personal network. Remember, all 50 of the producers who contributed to these statistics are successful, having produced at least four narrative features. However, all of the films you produce over your career are likely to earn more at the box office and receive more viewership if your biggest *equity* investor in your first film is from beyond your personal network.

Hopefully this chapter helps you begin to understand why independent film finance is so difficult. It is based on accounting and corporate finance, which are already complex, and then adds its own convolutions with the 120 and 50. This one chapter attempts to pack in the essentials from weeks of business school courses, so it would be smart to reread it to make sure you understand it as well as possible.

Takeaways

- You must have a basic understanding of the three main elements on the income statement (revenue, costs, and profits) and the three main elements on the balance sheet (assets, liabilities, and equity) to have an intelligent conversation with your potential investors.

- The risk-return tradeoff means that riskier investments must offer higher returns.
- The 120 and 50 structure allows independent producers to offer the potential for big returns to *equity* investors.

Notes

1 Cash includes physical currency and all of the money in the film's bank account.
2 If you're trying out the math on your own, you will notice that the price of the stock should be $6.20, not $7.87. The price of $7.87 is the price that the share trades on the stock market, which is determined by how much the investor's value the share. In contrast, $6.20 is called a book value, which is how much accounting rules say the share should be worth. If you want to get a better understanding of the difference between book value and market value, you can pick up any good financial accounting textbook. It's a huge topic with lots of debate, and well beyond the scope of this book.
3 This estimate is derived by a statistical technique called regression analysis. It attempts to measure how many more IMDB votes or how much more box office a producer would get over their career, all else equal. Even though some producers have more credits than others, some hold graduate degrees, some live outside of the Los Angeles metro area, and some went to film school, the regression analysis creates an apples-to-apples comparison despite all of those differences.

4 Debt Financing

> It's hard to get this information from producers.
> – Siena Oberman, producer

Chances are, you did not see *Valerian and the City of a Thousand Planets* in the theater in 2017. It only earned about $226 million in the global box office, mostly from outside the United States. However, what you missed was the theatrical release of the most expensive independent film ever made. Director Luc Besson indicated that the budget was in the range of $180 million. Let that sink in – he was able to make a $180 million independent film. The mechanism that allowed him to do that is debt financing.

You might take out a loan to help finance your film, which is a type of debt. Depending on which producer that you talk to, debt is either the one thing that makes film finance work, or the thing that they despise most. At some point, you will have your own experiences with debt and form your own opinion. In the meantime, I encourage you to experience it with an open mind.

In this chapter, you will see how debt works, understand the different types of debt, and get a peek at how producers used debt in their careers.

How Does Debt Work?

> It's just numbers. Eventually it will add up.
> – Carly Hugo, producer

Debt means that you borrow money to fund the production of your film, and are required to repay it with interest at some point in the future. The lender gives you cash to fund your movie today. Once your film generates revenue, you use some of that cash to repay the loan. Again, this is a case of money traveling through time. You do not have the money that you need to fund your budget, so you move the revenue back to the present with the help of a lender.

Remember the balance sheet from Chapter 3? When you take out a loan, your cash goes up by the amount that you borrowed (on the assets

DOI: 10.4324/9781003363446-6

side), while your debts go up by the same amount (on the liabilities and equity side). Both sides go up together, so your balance sheet still balances. If you borrow $100, the balance sheet might look like this:

Assets	Liabilities and Equity
Cash = $100	Loan = $100
Other Assets = $200	Equity = $200
Total = $300	Total = $300

As soon as a day passes, interest will be owed on the loan, and so that $100 loan value will increase. To keep the balance sheet in balance, either the assets need to go up in value or the equity needs to go down in value. (People typically borrow money to grow their business, so hopefully the assets go up!) Once the loan is repaid, the cash line goes down by the amount of cash used to pay it off, and the loan vanishes off the balance sheet.

Debt in Independent Film

There are essentially six types of debt, or six types of loans, that are used to finance independent films: negative pickup loans, presales loans, gap loans, mezzanine loans, tax incentive loans, and bridge loans. (Some aspiring producers have also tried selling their soul, but I do not recommend it.) They work as follows:

Negative pickup loans: If a single distributor agrees to pay for your entire production cost once the film is completed, that is called a negative pickup.[1] For instance, when George Lucas went back to work to make *The Empire Strikes Back*, it was allegedly financed with a negative pickup from Fox. Mr. Lucas' production company had to pay the full cost of making the movie, and then was repaid once it was delivered to Fox.[2]

In a negative pickup deal, the producer can turn to a lender to get a loan to fund production. The future payment from the distributor is a form of collateral. You can think of collateral as something that the lender gets to keep if a borrower does not repay their loan. For instance, that sweet new Tesla is the collateral on a car loan. (Car loans are bank favorites, because the collateral is already on wheels!) If the car buyer makes all of their payments on time, then eventually the loan is paid off and the owner keeps the vehicle. If they do not make the payments as promised, then the lender takes the collateral, sells it for cash, and uses the cash to pay off the money that is still owed on the loan.

Similarly, your lender is willing to let you borrow money to make your movie because they have faith in your collateral, just like with a car loan. A negative pickup contract from a reputable distributor is solid collateral. Your lender will require that the cash from the payment upon delivery goes to them first, not you or your film's other investors. (We will talk about how this works through a collection account manager in Chapter 11.) Your lender is willing to let you borrow money because they will get paid even if you do not personally pay the loan off.

Note that I am using the term lender here, not bank. A lender can be any person or company that loans money. Banks are one type of lender, that has to follow very special rules established by the government to be called a "bank." There are also non-bank lenders, which can be companies or wealthy individuals that have a pool of money that they loan out. Regardless of whether your loan comes from a bank or non-bank lender, you will sign a similar set of contracts to set up your loan. Be sure to have your attorney help you through them.

Negative pickups are one of the easiest ways to finance your film, and I hope you are so fortunate as to get a negative pickup deal someday.

Presale loans: While a negative pickup is meant to cover the entire cost of production, a presale agreement with a single distributor only covers a portion of the cost. These loans are tied to contracts that you and your sales agent negotiate with distributors before your movie enters production. Typically, your sales agent will bring your film to a market like the American Film Market or Cannes, to try to sell distribution rights.[3] This process normally happens once the script is near completion and key talent is attached. Various distributors from territories around the world will meet with your sales agent to hear the pitch. If you are lucky, one or more will agree to distribute your film. The contract that is signed to solidify the deal is called a presale contract, because it is happening before principal photography (thus, pre-) and because you are effectively selling the rights to distribute the film (thus, -sale).

Importantly, presale contracts always include a minimum guarantee, which is a fixed amount of cash paid to the producers (i.e. you) by the distributor when the completed film is delivered to the distributor. You will hear this called an MG. A minimum guarantee is a promise of revenue. Like the deal that the creators of *South Park* cut with Paramount Global, a minimum guarantee lets producers generate revenue before they incur production costs or make their movie. This is not just a trick reserved for the elite creators.

The key to making presale loans work is a minimum guarantee from a reputable distributor. There needs to be a promise of cash paid by the distributor to you once the film is delivered. If this minimum guarantee is promised by a distributor that the lenders trust, then you can borrow a portion of that money today.

In contrast, if you sign a presale contract with a distributor on the lenders' blacklist, then the lenders will not write a loan against it, and you will probably never receive that minimum guarantee either.[4] The lenders also avoid all distributors in economically unstable countries. Regardless of which distributor in Iran has agreed to pay you a fat minimum guarantee for your film, you will not be able to get a presale loan for it from a North American lender. The Iranian economy is too unstable, and that threatens the ability of all its distributors to pay as promised.

For fun, imagine that you strike a deal with a Scandinavian distributor that will guarantee a payment of $150,000 when you deliver the finished film to them. You can go to a lender and take out a loan so you can use some of that $150,000 today, but not all of it. Once the film is completed and the distributor pays the promised amount, that minimum guarantee payment should pay off your entire loan. If your film gets delivered to the distributor in under 18 months, there will probably be some money left over to pay your other investors.

There is a chance that the $150,000 minimum guarantee will not pay off the entire loan. That can happen if it takes longer than expected to deliver the finished film to the distributor. Presale loans typically assume that the film will be delivered within 18 months. Interest will build up within those 18 months, but the loan is structured so the amount borrowed and interest will be repaid entirely by the minimum guarantee. If it takes longer than 18 months to repay the loan, then the interest that is owed to the lender keeps growing and growing. If it takes four years to deliver the film to the distributor, the amount of interest due will have grown quite a bit, meaning that the amount owed on the loan will be more than $150,000, and the minimum guarantee will definitely not pay it all. The producers (i.e. you) will still owe the lender.

You do not get to borrow the entire $150,000 minimum guarantee. Instead, you get an advance rate, which is some amount less than the minimum guarantee. The rule in banking is that the minimum guarantee has to be bigger than the loan. Your minimum guarantee has to repay the loan, plus interest and the bank's transaction costs (the fees attached to the loan, attorney fees, the cost of the completion bond, and any other cost that gets rolled into it). One way that lenders compete is on the advance rate, or how big the gap is between the minimum guarantee and the amount of the loan.

Lenders also compete on interest rates and origination fees. The origination fee is meant to cover the lender's cost of setting up the loan, but is negotiable. If you shop around a bit, you will be able to compare lenders to find the best advance rate, interest rate, and origination fee for your film.

Borrowing money is expensive in part because of the interest, and in part because of all the transaction costs. When taking out a loan, you will need to pay both the bank's transaction costs and your own transaction costs. Your transaction costs include the cost of your attorneys, costs of processing paperwork, and arguably your time. Experienced producers have learned how to minimize these costs to get the most money out of their loans for their films.

If all goes well, you will end up with minimum guarantee-generating presales from lots of distributors around the world. Your lender will give you a separate loan for each distributor. If you add them all up, you might be close to achieving your financing plan.

* * *

When I am covering heavy material in the classroom, I find it helps to take a break and do something light and completely different to give the students' brains a chance to breathe. In that spirit, I would like to tell you a quick story about the making of my favorite father-daughter movie, *Beasts of the Southern Wild*. This story has nothing to do with debt, and is here just to give your brain a little rest, before we get back to the heavy stuff.

Producer Josh Penn will tell you that the way *Beasts of the Southern Wild* got financed was "an outlier and a fairytale, and not how you will get your first feature film financed." It was his first attempt at a feature. He and director Benh Zeitlin previously made a short film together called *Glory at Sea*, which was selected by South by Southwest and several other festivals. As he tells the story:

> At a festival nine months into its run, a financier saw it, loved it, and called to say, "We want to finance your first feature. Do you have something?" It actually ended up being real. We ended up being extremely well-aligned. We liked each other, and ended up making the film together. And we didn't even have a script at that point. And they found us, which doesn't happen with first features.

From there, the actual shooting of the movie sounds almost as magical as the film itself. Co-producer Matthew Parker describes it as his "most pure filmmaking experience." He recalled:

> We made up our departments of college kids who'd come in and heard about this adventure people were doing in Louisiana. There was a core group of people who stayed in the crew the whole time, but we had transient people show up for a week and be like, 'I like art' or 'I like electrical stuff' and we'd stick them in the art department or lighting. It was so far away from the norm. People were working six or seven days a week because they wanted to, for very little money. It was this beautiful experience. Everybody coming together to make this thing. It wasn't motivated by money.

And there was a great sense of community. In the off days, we'd have low country boils. We'd put newspaper down on picnic tables. We'd invite the community. They'd bring a Cajun band. We were integrated with the community and they all knew what we were doing, and it was a very cool thing.

The film went on to collect four Oscar nominations, including a Best Actress nomination for Quvenzhané Wallis (who is still the youngest ever nominee for the Academy Award). It also earned over $23 million at the box office, likely ensuring that all financiers got repaid. Both from a production side and a financial side, *Beasts of the Southern Wild* is the highest example of success in independent film. May you experience a similar level of success in your career.

Now, back to debt financing!

Gap loan: After you and your sales agent go through the process of trying to sell your film at a market, there will probably be some unsold territories. Maybe you will still be looking for a distribution deal in India, Italy, and Latin America. You might be able to get a loan backed by the expected sales in those geographies once your film is farther along. For instance, if your sales agent (who is wonderfully credible and well-known by the lenders) is confident that your film will earn at least $100,000 through distribution in India, even though no contract is in place yet, then the lender may be willing to provide you with a gap loan based on that $100,000 estimate.

Gap loans work almost entirely like presales loans, except that there is no actual minimum guarantee in place. Instead, the producer uses a guess about a future sale of the film to back the loan. That is a bit of an oversimplification that needs some unpacking. The guess comes from a sales agent, not the producer. Furthermore, it is not just a friend, walking into the bank, dressed up as a sales agent with a freshly-printed fake business card. This is a credible sales agent who wants to remain in the lender's good graces. The lender already has a long relationship with him, and he knows that the lender will only rely on his estimates if they are consistently reliable. His guess is a reasonable estimate of how much the unsold territories will eventually bring in.

As a result, there is much more risk for the lender, because the quality of your film suddenly does matter to them. If the movie turns out poorly, then it will not sell to distributors as expected, and the loan may not get repaid.

Hopefully you know enough about finance by now to know that bigger risks mean bigger interest rates. Your lender will charge you a higher interest rate on your gap loan than on a presale loan. Practically speaking, that means you will get to borrow even less on an expected sale of $100,000 than on an actual minimum guarantee of $100,000.

Your gap lender might be the same lender that issued your presale loan, or the funds might come from another source.

Mezzanine loan: If you have loaded up on presale loans and gap loans, and are still shy of making your budget, then you may look for a mezzanine loan, often referred to as mezz. A mezz loan is issued based only on the hope that the film will perform really well. There are no presales or expected sales to back it up. In order for a mezz lender to be repaid, all of the presales minimum guarantees must be paid on time, plus the gap loan must find more than enough additional distributors to buy the film. Mezz comes from lenders that are not banks, because it is way too risky for a traditional bank. As a result, the interest rates are higher on mezz than on gap or presale loans.

For filmmakers, mezz is really hard to get. I know of one mezz fund that looks at over 100 projects a year, and picks just two films to finance. In other words, there are over 100 movies a year that are really, really close to raising their financing plan, but are still short. Many are competing for those hard-to-find mezz funds.

In summary, mezz loans are expensive and difficult to get. However, they could also be the one last lump of cash to get your film into production.

Tax incentive loan: If you expect to collect a tax incentive from a government, then you can get a loan based on that too. These loans work almost identically to presale loans, because they are both collateralized. The presale loan uses the minimum guarantee as collateral, whereas the tax incentive loan uses the expected tax incentive payment as collateral. You also cannot borrow the full amount of the tax incentive, but instead get a lesser amount that ensures the lender gets repaid their interest and fees. We will talk more about tax incentives in Chapter 6.

Bridge loan: Imagine that your talent is signed on and ready to shoot for a limited number of days. Production has to begin before you lose them to another project. If you do not start now, you will be forced to recast your lead, your distributors and investors may back out, and the whole film could fall apart. You feel confident starting your principal photography because your presales loans are about to close and provide cash. However, you do not have the cash yet. What do you do?

The best tool to help you move forward may be a bridge loan. They provide a cash bridge from today until the other four aforementioned loans provide cash to the film. A bridge loan may last just a few days or weeks. They are repaid with the cash from the other four loans.

All of the four loans only provide cash to the producer once production has started. Presales, Gap, and Mezzanine all deposit the cash into the film's bank account after the first day of shooting, to ensure that the production is moving forward and the talent showed up as expected. Tax incentive loans often fund after three weeks of shooting, to ensure that enough money has been spent within the jurisdiction to earn the expected tax incentive. In the meantime, the producers still need cash to get through preproduction and the start of production.

The good news is that bridges are short-term loans, so there is not too much time for interest to build up. The bad news is that bridge loans are by far the most expensive, costing up to 2.5% per week in interest, because they are so risky for the lender. It is not unusual for a bridge loan to exceed a million dollars, so the actual weekly dollar cost can be $25,000 or more. Bridge lenders must accept all kinds of risks that the other lenders avoid. For instance, if John Malkovich is supposed to be on set on Day 1, and he is home with the flu and the whole production gets delayed, then the other lenders will still have their cash, but the bridge lender will be waiting and hoping the film still shoots. If it never shoots, the bridge lender may never get repaid.

That high borrowing cost means that bridge loans should only be used in case of emergency. Each dollar that pays interest and fees on your bridge loan is money being taken away from your production. Careful planning and execution is critical. Everyone on your team must be committed to getting the other loans closed in time so bridge loans can be avoided.

Bridge loans never come from banks, because banks like easily-manageable risks. You will likely get your bridge loan from a non-bank lender or from your equity investors.

Bridge loans allowed lots of great films to be made, such as Roland Emmerich's *Midway* and *Moonfall*. My alumnus, Thomas Mann, at the financier BondIt, explained that they are commonly used "because creative producers tend to underestimate the work required to close a multimillion-dollar debt deal." Clay Pecorin, producer of *Stowaway*, similarly notes that "traditional banks are slow." When your loans are taking too long to provide the cash you need, a bridge loan may save you. That said, you should approach them very cautiously and with a good, knowledgeable attorney.

* * *

The exact combination of loans that producers use for their films varies depending on the circumstances, more so than the producers' preferences. For instance, you can only use a presale loan if you have a presale. You can only use a gap loan if you have a film with a reasonable chance of earning more distribution deals in the future, on top of the existing presales. Tax incentive loans require shooting in a location with the promise of tax incentives. Mezz loans and bridge loans require lots of other financing sources to be in place. You will find lenders willing to work with you to build the optimal combination of loans once you have the right pieces in place.

None of these lenders are too hard to find. They need clients like you to borrow from them to stay in business, so they make themselves visible to the right people. You will find lenders at lots of industry events, working the room. If you are not able to get to the events, look at the speakers and panelists on the program. They are often lenders, trying to educate the filmmakers in attendance. (I almost always had a lender on my panel at the American Film Market, like my colleague Tony Beaudoin, because they are really good at explaining their part of the business.) Your attorney and sales agent also know the lenders who would consider working with you.

One thing that is certain is that you cannot call a lender and ask them to fork over the entire $2 million needed to make your film without other financial commitments on board. (Well, you can, but they will laugh at you.) You will not find a lender that will finance your entire picture without any other investors or collateral on your balance sheet. At a minimum, a mezz lender needs to see most of the financing coming from other sources. A presale or tax incentive lender needs to see the promise of minimum guarantees or tax incentive payments.

Debt in the Real World

Now that you understand the debt side of independent film finance, we can take a look at how it is used in the real world. Amongst the 50 successful narrative feature producers that I interviewed, only 16% were able to secure a presale for their first feature. Negative pickups were even more rare, with only 10% of producers signing such a deal on their first film, and all before 2002. By and large, the folks who received a presale or negative pickup on their initial feature project had a lot of prior work experience in the film industry. They often labored within a sales agency or distributor for several years, to build up an understanding of the market and what it takes to get a film sold. The data is pretty clear that presales are rare, and should not be expected to happen easily.

Debt is a really sophisticated financial instrument, and most producers only begin to use it once they build a track record of success. The average subject in my sample first used debt on their fourth feature film, and over one-quarter have still never used it. In many cases, producers went ten or more years into their career before financing a film with debt.

All of this is to say that you should not expect to start your producing career with debt-heavy films. This book talks a lot about debt, so that you understand what it is, especially relative to equity, and so that you understand how it works when the time is right in your career. I have heard a lot of panels and talks where aspiring producers are advised to just go out and get a presale on their films, but that is usually unhelpful advice. You will almost certainly start your career with equity-financed films, and then grow from there.

There is some evidence that producers who use debt sooner have more successful careers, but it is not conclusive. There are two ways to measure career success that I use throughout this book. The first is with box office, measured as the total worldwide revenue that the producer's films earn at the box office, as reported by Bruce Nash's the-numbers.com. The second way to measure career success is motivated by Maximilian Leo's taxi driver test in Chapter 1. To estimate the likelihood of a random taxi driver seeing the movie, I count the total number of votes for each film on IMDB. Presumably, the more votes, the more people who have seen it.

Now to the evidence. On one hand, using debt sooner does not significantly improve the box office performance of the producer's films. Amongst the subjects in my study, a producer who used debt on their very first film would have roughly the same lifetime box office as someone who first used debt on their 10th feature.

On the other hand, using debt one film sooner translates to about 11,300 more votes on IMDB over their career.[5] This result is a bit trickier to unpack, so I will go slow. Imagine we have two producers, who have each released four films. Producer A first used debt on their third film, whereas Producer B waited until their fourth. Given that Producer A used debt one movie sooner, we would expect all of her movies together to earn 11,300 more votes than Producer B. Here is where it gets more complicated. If Producer A first used debt on her second film instead of her third, that would put her debt usage two films ahead of Producer B. As a result, we would expect producer A to have 11,300 x 2 = 22,600 more votes than Producer B.

Using debt sooner may lead to greater viewership because debt relates to the commercial viability of the producer's films. Projects that raise money through debt tend to have bigger budgets, meaning that they have more money to spend on talent. For instance, amongst the second films made by the producers in my sample, those who used debt had an average budget of $5.1 million, whereas those who did not use debt only got to spend $3.6 million. The $1.5 million difference between those two groups could easily put a recognizable star in the cast and on the movie poster.

Collectively, the evidence suggests that using debt sooner in your career may not improve your lifetime box office but could increase the number of people who see your work. Probably the better reason to use debt sooner is that it helps you get your movies made.

Takeaways

- Unlike equity, debt must be repaid.
- Debt can be used to finance an independent film, but the lender will be looking for collateral.

- Riskier debts (mezz and bridge loans) will require you to pay higher interest rates than safer debts (presales and negative pickups).
- Debt is rarely used early in a producer's career.

Notes

1 Back when movies were shot on physical film, the cameras captured a negative image (whites were black, blues were orange, etc.) that had to be developed by a lab to make copies for the projectors in the theaters. If you owned the negative, then you could make as many copies as you wanted, so the negative was the most valuable finished product of production. The term negative pickup refers to that negative.
2 Mr. Lucas negotiated to maintain all merchandising rights to the *Star Wars* franchise in the deal, so while he had to front the production money, he made out like a bandit long-term with this savvy move.
3 If they bring you too, they will account for every dollar they spent on your travel, and charge the total amount back to the film as an expense. These expenses get recouped before you get repaid, once the film is released. They are not giving you a free trip.
4 The lenders' blacklist is not just a figure of speech or an idea. It is real. The community who will lend against presales contracts for independent films is small and they all know one another. When one lender gets burned by a distributor that fails to pay their minimum guarantee, they immediately notify all of the other lenders to update their blacklists.
5 This estimate is also derived by a statistical technique called regression analysis. It attempts to measure how many more IMDB votes a producer would get over their career, all else equal. Even though some producers have more credits than others, some hold graduate degrees, some live outside of the Los Angeles metro area, and some went to film school, the regression analysis creates an apples-to-apples comparison despite all of those differences.

5 Participation and Deferred Compensation

> The more the filmmakers and talent are compensated based on the success of the film, the more they are incentivized to make the film better.
>
> – James Short, producer

If your movie is going to make you rich – Fantastically Rich, RICH beyond your wildest imagination, RICH ENOUGH to support your heirs for generations – then it will be because of profit participation.

Mel Gibson's great grandchildren will never need to work a day in their life because of *The Passion of the Christ*. It is still the highest-earning R-rated film ever released in North America, and earned over $600 million theatrically worldwide. Mr. Gibson's profit participation was earned through his roles as producer, director, writer, and financier. I have seen estimates that he will earn in excess of $400 million from that one film. Even after paying attorneys, managers, agents, and taxes, he will have plenty left over to feed and house his family for years to come.

That $400 million is his share of the profits, also known as his participation or his back-end.

Mel Gibson isn't alone in this game. Robert Downey Jr. supposedly pocketed $55 million for *Avengers: Endgame*, Sandra Bullock allegedly earned over $70 million in participation payments from *Gravity*, Frank Darabont received over $200 million in back-end for creating *The Walking Dead*,[1] and many other actors, producers, and directors have hit the jackpot with monster hits that delivered huge profit windfalls.

In this chapter, I will explain how participation works, because it is important to you, your talent, and your equity investors.

To start, let's imagine that your film's income statement looks like this:

Revenue	$700,000
– Costs	$500,000
Profit	$200,000

DOI: 10.4324/9781003363446-7

If you made this film by yourself – financed it yourself, wrote it yourself, acted in all of the roles and directed yourself, then all $200,000 of profits would belong to you.

In the real world, a number of your collaborators are going to ask for a share of the profits. First, your equity investors will take about half of the pie (remember the 120 and 50 in Chapter 3). You get the other half to share with your writer, actors, director, and anyone else you choose. You begin the movie owning the entire pie, 100% of the profits, and then carefully give away slices until the movie gets made.

Each slice of the pie, each 1%, is commonly referred to as a point. If your lead actress gets a 10% share of the profits, then it would be correct to say that she has 10 points on the backend. (Maybe someday I'll start a band called Points on the Backend.) You can give away whole points, half points, quarter points, or any other fraction that you can imagine. You can also structure your points so that some points are paid before other points.

You can even go a step further and do what the studios do, creating different definitions of the word "profit" for each participant. There are two common definitions used in these contracts. The first is called gross profits, which is actually the revenue on the film's income statement or something very close to it, not profit. The second common definition is known as net profits, which is the actual profit line on the income statement (or something even worse when the attorneys get creative). A participant who is being paid 5% of gross profits will earn much more than a participant earning 5% of net profits. For example, if there were both a 5% gross profit participant and a 5% net profit participant on your film, the accounting would look as follows:

Revenue	$700,000
– Payment to Gross Participant	$35,000
– Costs	$500,000
Profit	$165,000
Payment to Net Participant	$8,250

The payment to the gross profit participant is more than four times larger than the net participant's. This example shows that two participants on the same film can earn different amounts, depending on the definition of profit used. The gross participant is paid earlier, and you will hear people in the industry describe this as being higher in the waterfall. (We will go much deeper into waterfalls in Chapter 11.) For now, you just need to understand that there are lots of ways to share the pie, and everyone who gets a piece of it wants their piece first.

As the producer, you need to carefully allocate the pie to make sure that the movie gets made, and with the optimal set of incentives in place for all parties. Participations incentivize your talent, your investors, and you in different ways, as I will explain in the pages that follow.

Profit Participation for Investors

Imagine walking into a sparkling new Las Vegas casino. That familiar casino smell isn't pervading the air yet, and the carpet is missing those one-too-many-free-drinks stains. Signs everywhere announce "Our slots pay back 7¢ on every dollar!" If you were smart, you would not play those slot machines – average slots pay out about 95¢ per dollar gambled. Losing 93¢ on every dollar that you put in is a good way to dump a cold bucket of water on a fun night. The only way you might play is if the casino was incredibly fun AND you knew that there was a chance you would go home with an astronomically, incoherently, unreasonably, irrationally huge jackpot.

So, not to be that cold bucket of water, but that is basically what your equity investors face when deciding whether or not to put money into the slot machine that is your movie. They know that the odds are very high that they will lose it all. Yet, they are hoping to have a fun time in the process and they keep hope alive for a jackpot.

That jackpot is their profit participation payment. Your equity investor will hand over a lot of money to you because there is a chance that your movie will pay them back more than they invested via participation. In other words, your equity investor is hoping to recoup their initial investment with a substantial amount of interest.

As you begin thinking about how to attract equity investors, remember that they are motivated by the chance of hitting the jackpot with your movie. You cannot promise them that they will hit the jackpot, because it is illegal to guarantee a return on a risky investment. However, you can show them all of the different ways they could gain value from their investment. We will talk more about how to do that in Chapter 12.

Profit Participation for Talent

There are two main reasons that you will want to give your talent a piece of the profit participation pie. The first is the performance incentive that profit participation creates. If your talent is just paid a flat fee, regardless of how the movie performs financially, then they lack the incentive to give it their all. Your actors may be unwilling to stay late to get the shot, take the risk that the director is asking for, or rehearse well to make sure everyone's performance is top-notch. Knowing that there is a financial reward for a good performance, the talent is incentivized to up their game.

Giving talent profit participations also puts them on the same page as the producers, financially speaking. Every expense puts the film's income statement farther from showing a profit, and therefore puts the talent farther from getting paid. Producers and talent alike are incentivized to contain costs to improve the likelihood of profit participation payments.

Profit participations also act as a form of compensation, but one that only pays out if the movie does well. Imagine that you are casting Emma Stone in your film. You have the option to pay Ms. Stone a flat fee of $30 million for her work, or you can pay her $20 million plus 20% of all profits. With participation, you need to raise $20 million to pay her. Without participation, you already need to raise an extra $10 million from your financiers. Your budget is higher, so it is harder to raise the capital needed to get your movie made, and pushes your project farther from becoming a reality. (Note that I am making up numbers here, and have no idea what Ms. Stone's fees are.)

But let's see how these two contract options play out under a couple of different financial outcomes, after the film is released. If the film is unsuccessful and never generates a profit, then you never have to pay Ms. Stone anything more. The profit participation option saves you $10 million!

If your film is successful, and it makes exactly $50 million in profits (not revenue), then Ms. Stone will get 20% of them, or $10 million. Once you add in her initial $20 million payment, the participation option pays her the same $30 million as the flat fee contract under this scenario. If profits are less than $50 million, you will have saved money with a participation deal. If profits are more than $50 million, who cares?! Everyone is making a ton of money, so go have a great party and enjoy it!

The right talent brings a lot of value to a film. Participation is one way to make sure that they are compensated for the value that they bring. It's also fair to say that key talent expect a profit participation. Even if you wanted to avoid paying back-end, you probably could not, because your lead actors, director, and writer will all demand some participation (or at least their attorneys will).

You can make anyone a profit participant. In Richard Linklater's *Boyhood*, there was a different song played for each year of the boy's life, to reflect popular music at the time. The film's total budget was only $2.4 million, meaning that the producers could not afford the rights to the songs. To get around that problem, all of the bands that contributed to the soundtrack – Coldplay, Arcade Fire,

Vampire Weekend, The Black Keys, The Flaming Lips, etc. – were compensated with participations. The film would go on to gross $48 million worldwide at the box office, and earn even more revenue other distribution channels, so all of the participants probably got paid.

I know of several films where everyone on the crew was paid union minimum wages plus participation. Even people who should have earned a decent wage, including the cinematographer, the unit production manager, and the production accountant (they're expensive, I promise) were all paid the minimum allowable amount. This permitted the films to be shot on very small budgets, with the bare-bones financial resources that the producers were able to cobble together from their financiers, and gave everyone a share of the up-side. I am certain that the producers who pulled off those shoots are successful today, because getting your entire cast and crew to agree to be underpaid is a remarkable bit of negotiating.

Even a company or a movie studio can be a profit participant. The DeLorean estate is now contracted to receive a share of the profits from *Back to the Future II* and *Back to the Future III* in exchange for allowing the use of the car as Doc Brown's time machine. I am also led to believe that Warner Bros. is a profit participant on the Disney film *Who Framed Roger Rabbit?* for the use of the Looney Tunes character Daffy Duck in a dueling pianos scene with Donald Duck.

In all of these cases, please note that I am saying that they *are* participants, not that they *were* participants. Participation is what is known as a perpetual contract, meaning that it never ends. As long as the film continues to earn profits, participants continue to get paid. At the extreme, profit participants on valuable classics like *The Wizard of Oz* and *Gone with the Wind* could conceivably continue to get paid today.

***

I want to come back to the idea that finance is about time travel. There is no requirement in law that one party pay another in the future. That is a choice. When the producer chooses to pay participations in the future, they are choosing to let their money time travel. Maybe they do not have the money today. Perhaps they have better uses for the money today. It is possible that they do not know how much to pay today, because they do not know the quality of the actor's performance, or the quality of the show, or how well it will be received by the audience. Regardless, the producer is choosing to pay the actor in the future, not the present.

Up through at least 2022, Netflix chose to not have their participation payments time travel. Instead of paying in the future based on performance, they paid in the present based on average historical performance of all movies. Only once cash transacts in the future, then we have finance, and that is why participation is an important part of film finance.

Profit Participation for You

There are likely only two ways that you will be paid on your films: a producer's fee and participation. Especially early in your career, your fee is going to be really close to $0, if not exactly $0. If you get paid anything meaningful on your earlier films, it could be because of participation.

Don't take my word for it. The Dear Producer blog commissioned a study in 2021 about producers' careers, called the "Producers Sustainability Survey Report."[2] They got over 500 producers to respond to their survey in the darkest part of the COVID-19 pandemic in late 2020. There are two quotes from it that stand out. "When asked what the lowest fee earned was, nearly 50% reported that they had taken no fee on at least one project." I promise it is not the big-time, successful producers taking no fee. They don't need to work for free. Their services are in demand, and they can find paying work. It is the early-career producers working for free.

Even if you successfully negotiate with your investors for a producing fee, "More than 80% have had to defer their fee at least once, with nearly 50% deferring their fee on multiple projects." Again, I don't think it is the successful producers who allow their fee to be deferred, it's the newbies. (We'll talk more about deferred compensation later in this chapter.) These two pieces of evidence combined suggest that early-career producers often work for free.

The odds of your participation making you rich aren't great. The same report showed over half of respondents never got paid a backend in the past decade. But, there is a reasonable chance your participations points will turn into cash. Forty-five percent of producers received a participation payment on at least one film, and about 1% were paid backend points on six or more films over the decade.

Participation gives you a lottery ticket, albeit with much better odds than Powerball. Like any lottery ticket, you should not make financial decisions or life decisions until after the numbers are called. Do not rely on participations to feed you, pay your rent, or put your kid through college. If you get a participations check someday, chances are that you will celebrate, enjoy, and get back to work, because it probably won't be that big.

Hollywood Accounting

The phrase "Hollywood Accounting" refers to a way to use creative accounting to ensure that participations and deferrals paid to talent are as small as possible. The creativity typically comes through the definition of profit used in the participation contract. When producers sign a participation agreement with talent or investors, they have the right to define "profit" in any way that they want, so long as both parties agree on the definition.[3] That is important – the calculation of profits must be clearly defined in the contract. There is no official, correct definition.[4] You now know that profit is just revenue minus expenses, so the important part is what gets included in revenue and what gets included in expenses.

If you are a studio or a producer, then you want the revenue as defined in the contract to be as small as possible. There are lots of tricks to make the revenue look smaller. One very common technique used by studio attorneys is to leave out revenue sources that have not been invented yet. Comedian Dave Chappelle famously signed a contract with Comedy Central for *Chappelle's Show* in 2003 that did not include the possibility of revenue from streaming services. Keep in mind, Netflix did not start streaming until 2007. The contract could have specified that revenue from all known and yet-to-be-invented technologies to distribute the show were to be included, but it did not. As a result, Chappelle earned precisely $0 in profit participation when *Chappelle's Show* was added to Netflix and HBO Max in 2020. All of the profits from selling the show to streaming services went to Comedy Central's parent, Paramount Global, instead.

Just as the studio or producer wants the revenue to appear smaller, they also want the expenses allowed in the participation contract to be huge. When *Goodfellas* producer Irwin Winkler sued Warner Bros. in 2015, his participation contract from that film became public record. In it, you can see that the studio slipped in a provision that allows them to charge interest to the film forever. Practically speaking, Warner Bros. earned back its investment in *Goodfellas* years ago. According to their internal accounting, the film only cost $34 million to make, and had earned $114 million in revenue. However, they were able to charge Mr. Winkler over $38 million in interest expenses in its first 20 years, because the contract said they could. The interest charges would continue to grow by over $800,000 per year, ensuring that the film would never be profitable. Without a profit, they could avoid paying Mr. Winkler a back end forever.

To be clear, the studios and producers do not want the actual revenue to be as small as possible and the expenses as big as possible. Their goal is for the contract to allow for the fewest, smallest sources of revenue and many, expensive sources of expenses, especially if they are fictitious. There was probably no point in time when Warner Bros. transferred cash to pay itself interest on its *Goodfellas* investment, so it is arguably a fictitious expense.[5] However, the contract allows it, so they get to include it in the calculation of profits.

Talent and investors want the opposite of the studios and producers – they want the profits as big as possible. Their attorneys fight to get every possible revenue stream included in the contract, and minimize the expenses.

There are so many tiny tricks that attorneys can use to tweak the definition of profit to the benefit of one party and harm of the other. For instance, I have a friend who agreed to a profit participation contract on a film they directed. They asked me to read it to find out if they were ever going to get paid. I was getting really excited reading it, because it seemed very favorable to the director. But then I found the one phrase that ensured that they would never get paid. The contract allowed the producers to include all expenses from their production company, not just the LLC that produced the film, in their calculation of profits. That means the producers could include development costs from other movies they made, rent, and any salaries they pay themselves to help ensure that the profits never exceeded $0. It was just a few words in one seemingly innocuous sentence that swung the whole profit calculation from positive to negative.

Giving away points and negotiating the definition of profit is not something that you should do without professional help. Make sure you have a good entertainment attorney advising you. You need someone who has written and negotiated hundreds of participation contracts, because those attorneys know how to avoid all kinds of problems. A good attorney at the front end will save you lots of legal trouble on the back end. (See what I did there??)

Deferrals Are Not Participation

Key talent on your film may get paid after your film is completed in two ways, participations and deferrals. Deferred compensation (also known as deferrals or deferments) means that some of the money that the producers are supposed to pay their stars does not get paid until the film has generated a certain amount of revenue.

For instance, on the Natalie Portman film, *Jane Got a Gun*, the director Lynne Ramsay contracted to be paid a directing fee of $750,000, with $300,000 of the $750,000 deferred until all lenders, labor unions, sales agents, and equity financiers had been repaid as contracted, and Natalie Portman and Michael Fassbender had received their deferred compensation.[6] In a pure accounting sense, deferred compensation is like the talent making an interest-free loan to the producers that only has to be repaid if the film is financially successful. If the film never earned enough money to repay the sales agents and equity financiers, then the producers would never have to pay Lynne Ramsay the $300,000 that she deferred.

Producers rely on deferrals because they reduce the amount of cash needed to be raised to fund the budget, and make it easier to hit the completion bonder's strike price. In the case of *Jane Got a Gun*, the producers needed $300,000 less to complete the film than they would have needed without Ms. Ramsay's deferral. Given that Natalie Portman and Michael Fassbender deferred some compensation too, the three combined probably deferred over $1 million.

Like participations, deferrals can be paid to some talent before others, as lead actors Ms. Portman and Mr. Fassbender were to be paid before Ms. Ramsay. It is also possible that two stars recoup their deferrals at the same time. Imagine Ms. Portman and Mr. Fassbender had each deferred $2 million. When a dollar of revenue comes in, each gets paid fifty cents on the same day. In the language that attorneys like to use, these payments are pro-rata and pari passu. The pro-rata part means that they each get their fair share, which is half in this case, because they are owed the same amount. (If Ms. Portman was owed three times more than Mr. Fassbender, she would be paid three times more, so she would get 75¢ and he would be given a quarter.) The pari passu part means that neither gets paid before the other. In contrast, Ms. Ramsay is not pari passu with these two actors because the contract clearly states that Ms. Portman and Mr. Fassbender get paid their deferrals first. She is also not pro-rata with them, because they get paid everything they are owed, before Ms. Ramsay is paid a single penny of her deferrals.

While deferrals are a wonderfully helpful tool for independent producers, they are not automatic. Talent must choose to defer compensation, and will only do so if they believe in the project. You cannot just go to Jennifer Lopez with an offer of $10 million, but $9.5 million deferred. Talent chooses to defer because they really want to see the movie get made, and they are willing to take the risk. It will be up to you and your attorneys to convince your key personnel to defer.

One other feature of Ms. Ramsay's contract is noteworthy here too. She was supposed to be paid after the equity investor recoups. On some films, deferrals are paid before equity, and on other films it is after. Everyone wants to be paid first, but that is not possible in the real world. Again, the order of payment priority is a matter for you, your investors, and your talent to work out amongst yourselves.

All deferral payments must be triggered by an event, and that trigger must be designed thoughtfully. I have seen contracts in which deferrals are supposed to be paid at a certain point in time, like the first day of theatrical exhibition, which is generally a bad idea. There is no guarantee that the producer will have the cash needed to pay the deferral when that time comes, and that can cause trouble. Instead, all deferred payments should be triggered by financial landmarks.

Rather than having the deferral pay when the movie is released, it is far better to pay when the film has generated enough revenue to repay the deferral.

Now we can tie participations and deferrals back to our discussion of balance sheets earlier. You may remember that the difference between liabilities and equity is the difference between owe vs. owned. Liability means money is owed, while equity creates an ownership position that only gets paid if the company makes a profit. A deferral is a liability, because the producers owe a fixed amount of money to the talent at a later time. A participation is an equity-like contract, because it only pays out if the film is profitable. The liability is safer than the equity because it gets paid first, but capped in the amount it can pay. The equity is riskier, but can pay *The Passion of the Christ* returns. When your director takes a deferral and a participation, she is receiving both liability and equity positions. She is hoping for a safe payment early in the waterfall and a jackpot later in the waterfall.

Do you remember that the folks that we call *equity* investors actually do the same thing? Earlier we talked about the 120 and 50. The 120 is a liability, equal to 120% of the initial investment. The 50 is half of the participation pie. *Equity* investors are combining a debt and an equity position in the waterfall, just like talent. This has evolved to be the way things work in film finance.

* * *

Participation may not feel like a fundraising tool, but it is. Giving your investors a share of the profits is an important enticement to get their commitment, and giving your actors a slice instead of an upfront payment reduces the amount of money that you need to raise to get your film made. You must incorporate participation in your financing plan because you have a limited profit pie to share. If your equity investors get 50%, then you only have 50% to share amongst your fellow producers and your talent, and it will disappear quickly if you are not careful.

Similarly, deferrals are an important fundraising tool. If you can convince your high-priced talent to work for a lower price now and more once there is revenue, then you reduce your budget and increase the likelihood of your film getting made.

This chapter gives you a quick overview of participation, but it is a really complex issue. The best book to learn more is the classic *Movie Money: Understanding Hollywood's (Creative) Accounting Practices*, written by Bill Daniels, David Leedy, Steven D. Sills, and Peter Klass. I strongly urge you to read it, as it is both entertaining and widely regarded as the best book about "Hollywood accounting" out there.

Takeaways

- Profit participation is one of the most important financial tools of an independent film producer to attract talent and investors, control costs, and reward success.
- Deferrals provide a separate means to reduce the amount of money needed to produce the movie by delaying payment until a certain hurdle has been crossed.
- Both must be negotiated and managed very carefully, and with professional help.

Notes

1. Yes, it is TV, but participation in TV and movies works the same way.
2. Read the whole, fascinating report at https://dearproducer.com/is-producing-a-sustainable-career/
3. The 2007 standard definition of profits used by Fox TV began with the following notice:
   THIS EXHIBIT "A" IS A CONTRACTUAL FORMULA FOR THE DEFINITION AND POSSIBLE PAYMENT OF CONTINGENT COMPENSATION WHICH PARTICIPANT ACKNOWLEDGES TO BE HIGHLY SPECULATIVE. WORDS AND TERMS USED HEREIN DO NOT CORRESPOND TO GENERALLY ACCEPTED ACCOUNTING PRINCIPLES ("GAAP") OR OTHER CONVENTIONAL UNDERSTANDINGS OF "PROFITS" OR "PROCEEDS" (WHETHER USED IN THE ENTERTAINMENT OR ANY OTHER BUSINESS). As a finance professor, I find it so funny that they put the word profit in quotes. Fox's attorneys chose to make it bold and all caps.
4. In the United States, the two most important financial agencies of the government use different definitions of profit. The Internal Revenue Service (i.e. the tax collectors) and the Securities and Exchange Commission (i.e. the financial regulator) have their own accounting standards, which do not always agree.
5. Please note that I am not using the term fictitious in a derogatory manner here. Proper accounting is filled with fictitious transactions, that all serve a meaningful purpose. If you know about depreciation in accounting, then you know a very common fictitious expense.
6. See United States District Court for the District of New Mexico, case number 1:13-CV-1075. The contract was revealed in a lawsuit after Ramsay allegedly walked off set. Mr. Fassbender was replaced at the last minute by Ewan McGregor. I don't know it to be true, but I hope Natalie Portman put on her Princess Amidala costume, and then pled with Mr. McGregor, "Help me Obi-Wan Kenobi. You're my only hope."

6 Tax Incentives and Soft Money

> OK, great, you're going to get several million dollars from the tax incentive, but you've got to find someone that needs it.
>
> – Judd Payne, producer

On the day after Christmas in 2014, my wife went to our local grocery store to pick up some diapers. While there, she saw a paper copy of the Los Angeles Times newspaper. The lead headline was "Filmmakers make movies with tax credits." Containing her excitement appropriately, she bought a copy and raced home to show me. If anyone thinks tax credits are boring and inconsequential, the *LA Times* disagrees! Front page! Lead headline! It was so gratifying to see my nerdy, niche interests getting the mainstream attention they deserve.

Tax incentives are worthy of the attention because they are so important to the creation of motion pictures and television shows. Each major studio collects more than $500 million in tax incentives in a year, or roughly the equivalent of Disney's profit from a massive global hit like *Black Panther*. Chances are, you will use tax incentives on your films too.

If you think back to the right-hand side of the balance sheet, you will remember that it shows the liabilities and equity of the film. Get ready for your mind to be blown – tax incentives are neither! Cash provided to the film by a tax incentive is neither a liability nor a source of equity. They belong to a class of financing known as soft money, which is money for your budget that never needs to be repaid to the source. Soft money does not appear on its own line on the waterfall side of the balance sheet, because it is technically revenue (the top line of the income statement).[1]

Producers want to use as much soft money as possible, precisely because it never needs to be repaid. This chapter will help you understand the basics of tax incentives, so you know where to go to find them for your film. It will also explore other types of soft money, including grants, crowdfunding, in-kind services, and that $1,000 from your grandma.

Tax Incentives

Christopher Nolan is one of my favorite filmmakers. I love his work, and I especially love his use of tax incentives. He is an absolute tourist, in the best sense of the word. His budget was supported by tax incentive money from the state of Illinois on *The Dark Knight*. He then moved on to claim money from the government of Alberta, Canada for *Inception*. Mr. Nolan followed up with additional stops and incentives in Iceland (*Interstellar*), the Netherlands (*Dunkirk*), Estonia (*Tenet*), and New Mexico (*Oppenheimer*). These locations, and their tax incentives, made his films better.

Tax incentives are a useful financial tool that essentially serves as free money that can support your budget. If you can earn tax incentive money from a government, then you do not need to raise as much money from your equity investors. As a result, a tax incentive makes your movie more likely to be completed.

This is not a secret. No government is hiding their tax incentives in a bunker where they can't ever be found. You do not need a special badge to get tax incentives. They are there for the taking, and producers of all stripes, all around the world, rely on these government programs to fund their movies. The important thing is that you have to spend money within the jurisdiction on production or post-production, and within their rules, to get paid.

State and local governments started implementing film production incentive programs in the late 1990s to attract good jobs. Plus, film productions are good for local economies. According to a study conducted by the United States Bureau of Economic Analysis, one film production job creates 3.35 jobs elsewhere in the economy. Those are the hospitality workers, who provide clean hotel rooms and warm meals to crews. Those are the hardware and craft store employees, who provide raw materials that get turned into sets, props, and wardrobe. Those are the production services staff, who manage rentals. All of those people then spend their money elsewhere throughout the economy to generate even more jobs. For politicians, attracting good jobs that create even more jobs is a big win.

The biggest winner of all is movie producers.

The way tax incentives work is typically by repaying a portion of the money spent on location. For instance, if you spend $1 million in the state of Georgia, then you get a tax credit of up to 30%, or $300,000, back from the state of Georgia. Your $1 million movie got much cheaper to make.

But this point is really important – in order to get a tax incentive, you must spend money in the city/state/country/jurisdiction first, and then you get paid back. They are also part of the broader income tax system, which means that there are lots of complicating rules and procedures that producers need to follow in order to get paid. Nonetheless, guaranteed money from the government is much easier to raise than equity from private investors.

There are two additional complications that come with that $300,000 from Georgia. First, you do not get a check for $300,000. Instead, you get a transferable tax credit. A tax credit is technically the right to reduce the income taxes that your film is obligated to pay based on the earnings of the film. (Remember, your film is a business, and might pay income taxes.) If your film owes income taxes of $500,000 in Georgia, then you can use this tax credit to reduce your bill, and your film will only pay the state $200,000.

Chances are, your film does not owe $300,000 of taxes in the state of Georgia, so the only way to turn your transferable tax credit into cash is by transferring it (i.e. selling it) to a Georgia-based company or family with a sizable tax bill. They will not pay you $300,000 for it, but a discounted price closer to 85% of that, or $255,000. In most places, producers do not get to keep the full face value of their tax incentive, because buyers will not pay the full amount. The purchaser of your incentive wants to protect themselves in case the tax credit does not pay off as expected, so that discount is like a little insurance.[2] A tax incentive broker will arrange the whole deal with the buyer for you. (Do not worry – reputable brokers are very easy to find with one internet search.)

The other complication related to this tax incentive is that you only get the money long after you complete your shoot or post-production work. You have to file the paperwork with the government with an accurate accounting of all of the money that you have spent in the location, wait for them to process it, and then find a buyer and complete the deal to convert your tax incentive to cash.[3] Depending on all of the mechanics, you may not see the money come back into your film's bank account until a year later.

This delay in receiving your tax incentive money means that you cannot directly use it to fund your production budget. Thankfully, a small industry has popped up that will loan you a portion of your expected incentive so that you can have some cash on hand to spend during principal photography and post. They will not lend you the full amount of the expected incentive, because they build in fees and interest, plus a safety cushion. They also generally will not fund the loan until at least three weeks into principal photography to ensure that enough money will be spent in the jurisdiction to gain the expected tax incentive. (This lender will often help you find a broker for your transferable tax incentive too.)

Some producers use their presale or negative pickup lenders to provide these loans, while others convince their equity investors to also be their tax credit lenders. For equity investors, getting to formally lend the tax incentive funds gives them another position that is higher up on the waterfall, and has a specific, government backed revenue stream attached to it. In other words, it gives the equity investor a safer investment to go with their risky investment. Whether your equity investor wants to back the tax incentive loan is up to them.

To summarize, tax incentives are the easiest source of financing to acquire, but come with the complications that they are only paid after production is complete and often must be sold at a discount. Tax credit lenders and brokers can make both of those complications easier to manage.

Georgia vs. the World

I intentionally began this discussion of tax credits with Georgia as my example, because the Peach State has the best incentive in the United States. Everyone who is anyone is shooting there because the incentive is so rich. Even Marvel shot huge chunks of *Avengers: Infinity War* and *Avengers: End Game* at Pinewood Atlanta Studios. In 2022, producers spent a total of $4.4 billion shooting 68 movies and 269 TV shows in-state.

The wonderful side-effect of all of that spending is that there is a well-trained crew base in Georgia and all of the production equipment a producer would ever need to rent. Producers can fly in their talent, and let locals do the rest of the work. There is no need to incur the expense of flying in and housing an outside crew. Note that the crew may not be any cheaper, because of union wage requirements.

One of the biggest reasons that so much money is spent on production in Georgia is that there is no limit on the amount of tax credits that the state can give out. While Georgia often hands out over $1 billion per year in tax credits to producers, California will only award $330 million annually, with only eight percent of that allocated to independent films. Additionally, the California credits are carefully rationed through an employment-based system, which means there is a slow, bureaucratic process to decide which movies will get the credits. Producers must wait to begin production until their application is approved by the California Film Commission, because spending that occurs before approval does not count towards the tax credit. In comparison, a crew can go to Atlanta and start shooting today, knowing that they will get a tax credit back from the state.

Georgia also does not limit the amount that it gives out per film. If a single picture spends enough to earn a $100 million tax credit, then the state will award it. In comparison, North Carolina will only pay out $7 million per film. If you have to choose between getting back $15 million from Georgia or $7 million from North Carolina, I am reasonably certain that you will choose to shoot your film in Georgia.

One issue that you might run into with the Georgia incentive, and many others, is that it requires a minimum amount to be spent within the state to get any money back. As I write this, the minimum is $500,000. In other words, if you only spend $499,999 on your shoot in Georgia, then you cannot get a tax incentive. If you spend $1 more, then you will get back $150,000 from the state. Minimums are generally in the range of $250,000 to $1 million. In New Mexico, there currently is no minimum, but you also cannot get a crew at this time, because Netflix has hired everyone. (There's a sentence that will be outdated faster than Quibi.)

To get the most bang for your buck, look for locations where tax incentives are stackable. For instance, the Canadian federal government offers a 16% tax credit on labor (or technically labour, because it is Canada). Producers are allowed to combine that with a 28% tax credit from British Columbia, to generate total tax credits of 39.5%. There are lots of rules that need to be followed to get both, but if you do, then the government is funding a huge chunk of your budget.

You cannot make your choice where to shoot solely based on tax incentives. There are no deserts or snowy mountains in Georgia. Your actors may refuse to work in Alberta. You may not be able to find the crew that you need in Minnesota. However, if you can make your production work in a locale with a rich tax incentive, then the odds of your film getting made go up considerably, because you will need to raise less money from investors to complete your budget.

It is also important to remember that tax incentives are just one financial consideration out of many. It is possible that you will spend more chasing incentives, between the cost of traveling your cast and crew, incurring higher labor costs, and other union considerations.

You also do not have to shoot in just one location. Many productions move some of their crew to various locations to capture multiple backdrops and multiple tax incentives. For instance, lots of shows will shoot just a handful of days in Washington, DC to get good exterior shots. The District's tax incentive is particularly constrained – they will only rebate up to $500,000 of payroll expenses per project. Still, it is better than nothing.

The one odd quirk that makes tax incentives slightly risky is that many of the laws written to establish local tax incentives also have built in sunset dates. Florida's incentive program was written with a sunset date of June 30, 2016, and was not renewed. Any productions that shot after that date would not be able to get a tax incentive from the state. You will want to do your homework with the help of a tax incentive consultant to make sure your film does not fall into that trap.

My favorite resource for tax incentives is the Entertainment Partners website, at ep.com. They provide easy-to-follow guidance on how much the incentive is in each locale, and what rules producers need to follow. In many cases, they also provide a link to the legislation or guidance that establishes the tax incentive, so you can read it yourself to get all the details.

Another good resource for tax incentives are film commissioners. They exist to encourage and enable film productions in their jurisdictions, so their job is to be helpful. Not only do they know the ins-and-outs of local tax incentives and grants, but they also know locations and permitting rules, the local workforce and service providers, and how to get the most out of shooting in their area. A simple internet search for any local film commission will lead you to the right contact information quickly. You can call them, email them, and find them at the major film markets and festivals. Get to know film commissioners early in your process to get the most out of their expertise.

There are lots of peculiar differences between the tax incentives offered around the world. If you use a resource like ep.com to narrow down your list of options, and then start talking with local film commissioners, you will be on your way to securing the tax incentive funding that your film is eligible to receive.

Nick Raslan offers really good perspective on tax incentives. He says, "sometimes going to the cheap place is way better than an incentive." To that point, when he priced out shooting *Queen of the Desert* in Morocco, he found it to be one-quarter of the cost of shooting in the New Mexico desert. The state tax incentive from New Mexico would not be nearly enough to bridge that cost gap. Tax incentives should be considered as one option of many to reduce the amount of money needed to shoot your film.

* * *

Earlier I mentioned that Georgia's tax incentive is a particular type called a transferable tax credit. Tax incentives can be one of four types: rebates, refundable tax credits, transferable tax credits, or non-refundable non-transferable tax credits. The differences are pretty technical, and not likely to alter your choice of where to shoot. Importantly, you do not get to choose which type to use. You pick a location to shoot, and then get whichever type that jurisdiction offers. Briefly, here are the key differences:

Rebate: This is a direct cash payment to the production company to offset production costs, and paid after the film's budget is spent. Rebates usually do not typically require the producer to file a tax return.

Refundable tax credit: Very similar to a rebate, but the film must file a tax return (just like you file your taxes with the government) in order to get the tax refund.

Transferable tax credit: This is the Georgia tax credit described above, and many other jurisdictions use this structure too. The film must file a tax return in the jurisdiction, and is able to sell the tax credit to another party.

Non-refundable non-transferable tax credit: This is a tax credit that can only be used by the production company to offset taxes due on profits that the production company earns. It cannot be used to generate a tax refund (thus, non-refundable) and it cannot be sold (thus, non-transferable).

Grants

Tax incentives are not the only form of soft money available to help fill your budget. Grants also provide cash to filmmakers that rarely needs to be repaid. While tax incentives are often paid after the film is finished, grants can land in your bank account before you start shooting. As a result, you will not need a loan to help your grant time travel, unlike a tax incentive. Cash from a grant is technically revenue (on the income statement), so the grant is not in the waterfall.

Grants originating from within the United States are primarily intended for producing documentaries, but overseas grants are often viable for funding narrative films. The producers that I interviewed told me about grants they had earned from the governments of Australia, Canada, Germany, South Africa, Spain, the United Kingdom, and the European Union. There are endless differences in these programs, but most were accessible to foreign producers for narrative features. Usually, to get funding as a foreigner, there needs to be a citizen or group of citizens connected to the project. For instance, Stuart Pollok received a sizable development grant from the government of Wales for *One of the Hollywood Ten*. Mr. Pollok is Scottish and his producing partner was Spanish, and yet they were able to qualify for the funding because their director, Karl Francis, was Welsh. The money they received from the Welsh government allowed for Mr. Francis to be paid to develop the script, which was critical to getting the film made.

Producer Diane Quon may be the modern master of grants. She earned grant funding from foundations on her first six documentary films, including the Oscar Best Documentary Feature nominee *Minding the Gap*, all within a period of six years. Ms. Quon's advantage may be that she spent 17 years in marketing, first at NBC, and then at Paramount. The business of marketing is selling to an audience, and she keenly understands how to do that in a grant application. The tricky thing with grants is that you need to think about two audiences in your proposal: the film's viewers and the grant reviewers. Ms. Quon told me that the reviewers, "want to believe in the director. They want to see that they're story tellers." Even though your director is a visual story teller, the grant application has to tell a written story too.

Ms. Quon insists on being as clear as possible about the story in her applications. She and her director work to figure out the three acts of the story, and then they describe them in the proposal. If they have key quotes from their existing footage that drive the story forward, they include those as well. All of this effort helps create a picture in the reader's head, so they can imagine the movie for themselves. Ms. Quon admits that it is hard to know the ending or what they want the film to say at that early stage, but it helps to think of this work as a first draft.

Grants are perceived to be a difficult form of financing because they take time. For instance, from the time that you apply for a funding from the Arthur Vining Davis Foundation to the time that they deposit the cash in a bank account will be a minimum of 10 months. However, you may spend just as long, if not longer, trying to find a financier for your project. The best approach to raising money is to chase both at the same time. Only once in my interviews did I hear a producer say that they had too many investors wanting to contribute. You should be hunting for grants, equity investments, and all other forms of capital simultaneously.

It is unlikely that grants will fund your whole budget, or even a majority of it. Documentarian Alessandra Pasquino optimistically told me that "grant awards certify that (your movie) is a good idea for other investors." She finds that equity is easier to raise once an independent body like the Catapult Film Fund puts their stamp on one of her projects.

The available grants on the market are constantly changing. Last I checked, filmdaily.tv maintained a nice, freely available list of grants around the world.

If you are hoping to receive a grant from a nonprofit foundation in the United States, there are lots of rules and limitations that you need to be aware of. For instance, most grants can only be paid to legally registered nonprofit organizations, not people. That means that you may either have to go through the process of setting up a nonprofit or finding a fiscal sponsor.

A fiscal sponsor is a non-profit organization that is able to accept grant money on your behalf, even if you are making a for-profit film. They do not do this work for free – they will take 5% to 15% of your grant money as an administration fee. To be fair, they have a lot of work to do to qualify as a fiscal sponsor and accept money on your behalf, so this fee can be a good deal. Some experts suggest that you will save money using a fiscal sponsor instead of setting up a nonprofit if your budget is less than $2 million per year (not per film).

Just like you need to find grants that match the goals of your film, you will also need to find fiscal sponsors that match the goals of your film. Otherwise, they legally cannot sponsor you. Some organizations, like Film Independent, can sponsor virtually any film. Others can only support films that meet their narrower missions, such as Women Make Movies. Either way, fiscal sponsors now offer an amazing array of services to help your financing goals, including credit card processing. Check out amdoc.org for a helpful listing of current fiscal sponsors.

Another benefit of using a fiscal sponsor is that your contributors can decide whether they will be a donor or an investor. If your film is a nonprofit, you cannot have investors and you cannot personally benefit from any profits that the film generates. If your film is for-profit, then you can have both donors and investors (and profit participants). Some people like donating because it helps them pay less when their income taxes are due in April. Others want the ability to earn a return on their investment, and prefer to be an investor.

Attorney and producer Todd Burns fully understands the power of using nonprofits to help finance his films. His credits to date include *Machine Gun Preacher* with Gerard Butler, and the intense *The Stoning of Soraya M*. Throughout his life, Mr. Burns has started dozens of nonprofit organizations to support his social causes. He recently mentored and represented a documentary about hook up culture, *Liberated*, that was sold to Netflix. The funding to make the film came from a nonprofit organization that he started to advance the cause of liberating trafficked persons. The nonprofit raised money from a wide net of donors, and then used those funds to support the film that aligns with its mission. To be clear, the nonprofit that Mr. Burns helps run is paying for the movie, and this is totally allowed. The donors know and support it, and for good reason. As a result of the investment, the nonprofit is an equity financier in the film. Here's where it gets really good: when the film sold to Netflix, the nonprofit got all of its money back plus a profit. In addition, they accomplished their mission of raising awareness of their issue on a global platform, which is their charter. Through this structure, Mr. Burns killed three birds with one stone. He produced his movie, accomplished his social mission, and provided money to his nonprofit to keep their work going!

Other Soft Money

Crowdfunding on sites such as Indiegogo, Kickstarter, and Support Our Story also provides soft money that you can use to complete your budget. These work by letting entrepreneurs announce their project and fundraising goals, and letting the crowd contribute online. In exchange for using their platform to announce your project and collect money, these services will take a small percentage of the contributions that you received.

Usually there is an incentive involved for the donor. For instance, if someone contributes $20, they might get a digital copy of the script.

In exchange for a $100 contribution, maybe they receive a paper copy of the script, signed by the director.

If you promise to provide signed scripts, digital downloads, actor meet-and-greets, or anything else in exchange for cash on a crowdfunding website, then you are legally obligated to meet your promises. Entrepreneurs have been sued by state attorneys-general for failing to meet their crowdfunding commitments. You should think of all of those commitments as liabilities on your balance sheet until they are paid off, because that is how the government views them.

The first day of fundraising on a platform should be the culmination of the campaign, not the start of the crowdfunding. Campaigns are successful when all promotional materials are ready at launch, a strategy to gain and maintain engagement is ready from day one, key funders are ready to donate a significant portion of the goal in the first hour, and a list of at least 5,000 viable donors/fans is ready to be contacted to announce the launch. It takes a lot of work before the campaign ever goes live to make it a success.

This may be the last time that I talk about crowdfunding in this entire book, because it has largely gone out of favor. I rarely hear anyone talk about it anymore. Only two of the producers that I interviewed raised money through crowdfunding. *Roll with Me* producer Lisa France told me that she needs a six-person team to manage a crowdfunding. The reality is, your movie is probably going to be better if those six employees are making the movie, instead of running a fundraising campaign.

In-kind sources are also soft money. The phrase in-kind means that someone is paying with goods or services, not money. If you get free use of a camera, an editing bay, or a location, that is an in-kind contribution to your budget. Similarly, getting products for free in exchange for showing them on screen provides another source of soft money. This type of product placement happens frequently in independent films.

One producer I interviewed told me about getting scammed out of A LOT of money through in-kind soft money deals. The scam began with a production services company signing a contract pledging to give the producer free equipment rentals and services in exchange for a credit on the film. They claimed to be a new company, just trying to get their name out there in the business. The contract had a cap of $100,000 of soft money, meaning that the production services company would not charge for the first $100,000 of costs, but the producer would be required to pay any costs over that limit. To celebrate the agreement, the owner of the production services company took everyone out for a fancy dinner with lots of expensive wine. The bill was over $4,000. Guess what? The contract allowed him to count that dinner as part of his $100,000 contribution. At the end of the shoot, the producer was given an itemized statement showing all of the costs for all of the rentals, services, and the fancy dinner, and the total far exceeded $100,000. The producer had no choice but to raise more money to pay the tab. Luckily, the producer was able to raise more money, and did not have to abandon a partially completed film.

To make matters worse, this was the second time the producer had been scammed by this type of deal. In both cases, the contracts were vetted and negotiated by the producer's skilled attorney, and the producer still ended up with a bill for tens of thousands of dollars. These are not a rare occurrence.

The best way to avoid such scams is to avoid in-kind soft money from production companies that do not have film or television credits yet. Often these companies only operate for a short time, and then change names so you cannot find the films they worked on in the past. If you have an in-kind offer from a company with credits, talk with the producers who worked with the company on a prior shoot, to make sure you won't get stuck with a huge bill at the end.

Let's end on a positive note. Soft money is possibly a tool that you will use on your first film. Amongst the producers the I interviewed, about 37% used a tax incentive or grant on their first film. The majority of my sample had received soft money funding by their second film. There is evidently a good support system in place to help you earn soft money, and I hope you will take advantage.

Takeaways

- Tax incentives provide cash that never needs to be repaid, but you have to carefully follow the government's rules to earn it.
- The money from a tax incentive is received after production finishes, so you will need a lender to help it time travel if you want to use some of the funds for production.
- Grants are another valuable form of soft money and are more helpful with documentaries than with narrative features in some countries.
- In-kind soft money can help reduce the amount of cash needed to be raised but beware of scams.

Notes

1 Soft money provides cash that increases the assets side of the balance sheet. To keep the balance sheet in balance, then the equity must go up too.
2 In cases in which the state later finds fraud in the tax incentive filing, they can cancel the incentive.
3 You might need to hire a specialized accounting firm like Brauer & Co. to help with the paperwork.

7 Budgets

> Try to make movies at a reasonably low price.
>
> – Bill Borden, producer

I work at a small university that is basically an extension of the Catholic Church. We are a nonprofit, that happens to spend around $400 million each year. We pay about 1,000 professors, maintain over 50 buildings, award scholarships to thousands of students, and do all of the other costly things that colleges do. If we did not have a plan for how to spend that $400 million each year, we could not survive. In other words, we begin each year with a budget.

Budgeting is the financial foundation for all sophisticated organizations, regardless of whether they are huge corporations, nonprofits, or governments. All of these entities use budgets to allocate their money wisely and ensure that they do not go bankrupt. After all, a budget is really just a best guess of the costs on the income statement. Companies figure out how much they can spend on their employees, buildings, and marketing each year by estimating how much revenue they will have coming in. The same should be true of independent films too. Your budget definitely should not exceed the amount of money that you expect your film to generate.

This chapter will give you an overview of budgeting issues in independent film. You will get budget advice for your first film and learn about the budgeting issues that arise when working with lenders and labor guilds.

First Film Budgets

> Trim your budget to the bone.
>
> – Tom McNulty, producer

The most important advice I can offer in this chapter is to make sure your budget is as small as possible on your first film, for three reasons.

First, the smaller the budget, the more likely the film is to get made. It is much easier to find people to give you $100,000 than $1 million.

In fact, according to the United States Federal Reserve Survey of Consumer Finances, there are about ten times more households with a net worth over $1 million than households with a net worth over $10 million. In other words, by aiming for a lower budget, you can expand the pool of potential investors by up to ten times.

Second, the smaller the budget, the smaller the sliding-scale costs. These are costs that get bigger as the budget gets bigger. For instance, there is a sliding scale cost to houses: the bigger the house you buy, the more it costs you to heat it in the winter. (I think there is also a sliding scale cost to a night out: the more you enjoy yourself, the worse you feel the next day.) The completion bond, insurance, and wages are all sliding-scale costs, because all get bigger as the budget gets bigger. The completion bond and insurance are priced as a percentage of the budget. The stars in your film will ask for more if they know the budget is bigger (or, their agents will). If you are shooting within the jurisdiction of a guild, like SAG-AFTRA, then they set a minimum that all on-screen talent must be paid, which increases as the budget increases. Keeping your budget down keeps your sliding-scale costs down too.

Finally, the smaller the budget, the bigger the upside for you and your investors. If your film is a hit on a big budget, there might not be much money left over after paying off the production cost. If your film is a hit on a small budget, you'll be able to live comfortably and your investors will be happy.

When Seth Caplan was gearing up to tell me the financial story behind his animated short, *Flatland*, I'll admit that I was ready to be underwhelmed. This book is really about features, and I've never heard of a short that was a financial success. You probably read the book *Flatland* in a high school math class, about characters stuck in a two-dimensional world. Mr. Caplan and his partners made the movie on a shoestring budget, while casting voice acting from amazing talent including Martin Sheen, Kristin Bell, and Tony Hale. The producers knew they had a built-in audience of math teachers, who would show *Flatland* in class to their students (thus the reason it had to be shorter than feature length). They also knew they could charge more for each copy sold or licensed to a school than a typical feature, because each school would be showing it to hundreds of students. To date, *Flatland* has been seen by over a million high schoolers. It also returned nearly twenty times its budget. The producers keep getting paid each year, the actors keep getting paid each year, and the happy investors keep getting paid too. All parties are still making money on it because the budget was so low. With his earnings from *Flatland*, Mr. Caplan has been able to get several other films off the ground. The one thing better than a beloved film is a beloved film that is a financial success.

Especially for your first film, it is really important that your investors get their money back. If they do, chances are they will invest with you again, and so will their friends. This type of win gives you a positive financial track record, and demonstrates to other financiers that you have what producer Eric Fleischman calls "a commercial mindset." Legendary producing mentor Gill Holland was a bit blunter. He told me, "if that first film had not been a financial success, I don't know if I could have made another."

Amongst the 50 narrative producers that I interviewed, the smallest budget for a first feature film was $4,000. Nearly half of the first-films released after 2002 had a budget under $500,000. There is no shame in starting small to get a producer credit under your belt. As *Mainstream* producer Siena Oberman suggests, "build a good reputation doing smaller things."

The average first film budget amongst my producers was $2.9 million. Their second films are a bit bigger, with the average spending approaching $4.3 million. Amongst the 33 producers who were willing to share, the budget on their most-recent film was nearing $11.2 million. One important takeaway from these statistics is that producers get to work on bigger projects as they achieve certain levels of success. Starting with a smaller budget does not mean you will always have a smaller budget.

Keep in mind, small budgets mean tight shooting schedules. When *Margin Call* was shot in 18 days in 2010, back when 36-day principal photography schedules ruled, producer Rob Barnum tells me that "people were jaw-dropping shocked." The norm for indie shoots now is 18–22 days. Being able to pull off your first film that quickly will go a long way to convince financiers that you are up to the challenge of a bigger film.

* * *

Film budgets are intricately difficult and require people with great skill to build them right. You definitely cannot learn how to craft a budget in one chapter of a book. If you want a rock-solid budget for your film, hire a good line producer. The job of the line producer is to shoot the film within budget. They can estimate how much it will cost to produce your project based on their years of experience in the field. Line producers also know hundreds of clever strategies to control the budget. Their estimates will be both credible to your investors and reliable to you in your planning.

From your potential investor's perspective, a budget is critical. A film budget is a projection of how much money will be spent to make the movie. If you are going to raise money for your movie, you need to know how much to raise. After all, there is no need to raise $10 million when you can make it for $2 million.

Budgets can differ widely from reality. Your movie's actual cost can go over budget in many more ways than you can ever imagine. For instance, when the producers began production with a $60 million budget on the Alejandro Iñárritu film *The Revenant*, they had no idea that they would run out of snow in Canada. As a result, they had to move production to Argentina to finish the winter scenes they needed. In the process, the shooting cost ballooned to $135 million. All experienced producers have had a budget miss the mark due to unforeseen expenses, like talent refusing to perform, overtime, or reshoots. Budgets are never perfect.

It is wise to have a conservative budget to help you cope with uncertainty. (Hopefully you never have uncertainty like that!) The worst thing that you can do to your investors and for your career is spend a boatload of money on a movie, and then run out of funds before it is done. There are thousands of unfinished movies sitting on hard drives around the world at this moment, that will never get completed and never be seen by audiences. All of their producers can tell you that it is a position that you never want to be in. You must build your budget in such a way that you can finish your movie even if trouble arises.

Before reaching out to investors, make sure your budget is nailed down. It should specify all that you need to spend to get the film completely through post-production. If you want to pay yourself, include a producer's fee in there too (although your investors will almost certainly ask you to reduce it, defer it, or remove it). Work with a line producer to get it right.

Bonds, Insurance, and Deposits

If you are borrowing money from a lender, then you may also be required to get a special kind of insurance called a completion bond. These bonds ensure that your film gets finished and delivered to distributors so that the promised revenues can be collected. If needed, the completion bond company can put in their own money to get the movie through to delivery. They can also fire everyone on the production, including the director and you, and take over.

Completion bonds carry two important costs that affect your budget. First, your completion bonder will require you to raise 10% more cash to have on hand than your budget requires, which is known as a budget contingency. (For instance, if your budget is $1,000,000, then the completion bonder will require you to raise $1,100,000 before you can begin production.) The budget contingency will be built into the strike price, which is the amount that the completion bonder believes will be needed in order to complete and deliver the film. If you do not raise an amount of money equal to your bonder's strike price, then you will not be able to get the completion bond. Second, the completion bond fee may cost you 7–15% of your budget. Between the two, a completion bond will force you to raise 17–25% more money from investors than if you did not have one.

While they sound scary, my personal opinion is that completion bonds are often great, and many films could benefit from being bonded. A budget contingency is not really a cost – it is smart planning. Even the Documentary Producers Alliance (DPA) suggests that, "All budgets should include a contingency to account for unforeseen expenses reasonably expected in the production process (commonly up to 10%)."[1] The completion insurance provided by the bonder is a comforting feature for equity investors too.

On top of those benefits, the completion bonder effectively is required to provide budget consulting services to the film. In order to insure the film in the first place, the bonder must go over the script, shooting schedule, and budget with a fine-tooth comb, to ensure that the budget is sufficient. Bonders know budgets well. They spend their days reviewing an avalanche of them and observing whether there was enough money to complete the shoots. If there are problems with your budget, your bonder will find them. Finally, the completion bonder is an effective "bad guy," to help get the producer, director, production manager, and investors all on the same team.

The size of the film is often the barrier to getting a bond. The legal fees to secure a bond are in the vicinity of $80,000, so on smaller projects, the cost may not make sense. However, there is no minimum budget. Completion bonders will take films of all sizes.

While completion bonds are one kind of insurance, they are not the only insurance that your film will need. You also need to budget for film production insurance. These policies will protect the film from a wide variety of mishaps, including deletion of a hard drive, injuries to cast and crew, and damage to equipment, vehicles, sets, and props. Traditional business policies, including worker's comp and E&O (errors and omissions) are needed for each film too. There are specialized brokers who can help you get the right policies, but they all come with a cost that needs to go into your budget.

When Paul Walker tragically died while *Furious 7* was being shot, insurance helped mitigate the financial fallout. Universal Pictures paid for an insurance policy with Firemen's Fund before production began. Upon Mr. Walker's death, the insurer had the option of either repaying all of Universal's expenses and abandoning the film, or paying the additional costs to finish the film without their star. The additional costs included reshoots of certain scenes, and a lot of visual effects to insert Mr. Walker's face on his brothers' bodies. Thankfully, they chose to finish the film, fans showed up to see it in theaters, and Universal did quite well financially.

One other cost that early-career independent film producers often do not include in their budget is SAG-AFTRA production deposits. If your on-screen talent is covered by the actors' guild, then you will need to make a deposit in the amount that SAG-AFTRA tells you (usually about 40% of expected wages). The purpose of this fund is to ensure that the actors get paid, even if the production runs out of money. None of this cash actually goes to pay the actors, assuming you make payroll on time, so it is just money sitting around until SAG-AFTRA decides to give it back to the production after it wraps. Instead of raising money to pay 100% of your actors' wages, you need to raise about 140% of their wages from your investors.

Takeaways

- Work with a line producer to build an accurate budget that includes all necessary costs.
- Keep your budget as small as possible on your first film and go bigger as your career grows.
- Allow yourself some wiggle room in your budget for the unexpected.

Note

1 See the DPA's 2020 "Guidelines for the Documentary Waterfall" at documentary.org.

8 Four Paths to Funding Your Budget

> The only way to get backend is to make it on spec.
> – Judd Payne, producer

Now that you understand the basics of film finance, we can dive a little deeper into the practicalities.

Practically speaking, there are only four ways to fund your budget: cash-flowing, negative pickups, presales, and on spec. This chapter describes each, and provides insights into their prevalence.

Cash-flowing is a term used to describe a company's use of cash-on-hand to pay all costs of making the film, as those costs happen. For instance, when the Walt Disney Company makes a Marvel film, they cash-flow it. Disney does not go out and raise debt and equity to make the film. They just take cash out of their bank account as needed and pay the costs.

Similarly, production companies and movie studios occasionally will cash-flow independent producers' projects. These are often referred to as PFD deals, standing for production, financing, and distribution. The producer does not need to raise outside debt or equity for the production of a cash-flowed film. The entity providing the cash-flow typically owns all distribution rights to the film in perpetuity and a significant portion of the equity. The producer is paid a fee for their services, and occasionally receives a small equity stake in the film.[1]

We talked about negative pickups in Chapter 4. They are a little more complicated than cash-flowed movies, because the producer still has to go get a loan to provide the cash for the production. Negative pickups are still a very easy way to finance a film because there is only one lender and no need to find equity investors to fund the production.

Presales are also covered back in Chapter 4. In a presale, the producer sells the rights to distribute the film to several international distributors before it is finished, in exchange for a promise of payments when the film is completed. As in a negative pickup, the producer uses the contracts as collateral to get a loan. Presale financing is more complicated than negative pickups because there are many parties and many lawyers all over the world involved.

DOI: 10.4324/9781003363446-10

Four Paths to Funding Your Budget 79

The riskiest path is making your film on spec.[2] On spec films use equity to finance most or all of the budget, when there is no contract in place to distribute the film before production begins. Producers of on spec films can raise capital through tax incentives, grants, and crowdfunding, and often use deferred compensation to attract key talent. These movies are made in the hopes that they turn out well, and buyers will then emerge for their distribution rights. The key financial risk with on spec films is that the investors lose everything if no buyers emerge.

If there is any way to avoid it, do not make your movie on spec. In his classic book, *The Biz*, legendary attorney Schuyler Moore insists that you should, "Never, ever, ever start production without locking up distribution in advance" (pg. 13).[3] Especially in today's film world, where there are so many movies being made, you put your project and your investors at a huge disadvantage if you make your movie on spec.

Each of the four ways to fund your budget described here are tied to distribution. Cash-flowed, negative pickup, and presold films all have some funding from a distributor before production begins. Films made on spec do not. All of these can have additional equity investments too, to complete the funding.

With all of that said, now is a good time to peek at the data to see how first films fund their budgets. Amongst the producers that I interviewed, the majority (73%) made their first film on spec. Despite this number being surprisingly high, you should think of it as a low-ball estimate, for two reasons. First, I only interviewed successful producers, who made at least four films. Many more films are made on spec by first-time producers who never get the chance to make a second movie. Second, a number of the producers that I spoke with began their career before 2002, when straight to VHS negative pickups and cash-flow deals were very common. Amongst the producers who made their first film after 2002, 79% of first films were made on spec. The real number is certainly higher than 79% today. While making your first feature on spec is incredibly risky, it seems to be the path that most producers are forced to take to jump-start their careers.

Just to put a bow on the math, the other 21% of films were made with some presales in place. On average, the presales on those first films paid for 77% of the budget. The producers of those films largely had considerable production, sales, or distribution experience prior to making their first films, which gave them the right connections to earn presales. The key takeaway is that it is possible to avoid making your first movie on spec, but only if you carry an exceptional set of work experiences and connections. We will talk more about how experience affects financing in Chapter 13.

On one hand, I really must advise you to never make a film on spec. The streamers rarely buy films made on spec, preferring to have a hand in the development process. There is little theatrical market for indies anymore, so your chances of generating revenue from the box office are very small. You practically have to hope for a magical film festival run followed by a bidding war for the rights to your film, which is really rare. The odds of a film made on spec getting a release and repaying investors is small.

On the other hand, so many producers began their career by making their first film on spec. It seems that making a film on spec is a rite of passage for new producers. If you are going to make a film on spec, keep the budget small to minimize the risks to your investors, and make it look as good as you possibly can.

I began this chapter with Judd Payne's assertion that "the only way to get backend is to make it on spec." Films made on spec are the riskiest, so they also have the highest upside. If the film turns out amazing and there is a bidding war, then the financiers and producers can earn life-changing returns through their participations. However, participations can pay out in presold films too, if they perform well theatrically. The minimum guarantee in the presales contract, as the name indicates, is just the minimum amount that the distributor will pay the producer.[4] If the film generates enough revenue to trigger payments beyond the minimum guarantee, then the distributor will be contractually required to continue sending cash to the filmmakers and investors. In those cases, the producer could earn participation payments too. Life-changing bidding wars for on spec films are rare, and life-changing theatrical runs for presold films are rare. Don't count on either, but I hope you get to enjoy at least one in your career!

Takeaways

- Your budget will either be funded by being cash-flowed, through a negative pickup, with presales, or it will be made on spec.
- While making films on spec is riskiest, it is also most common for first films.

Notes

1 One particularly experienced interview subject noted that producer fees on films with budgets in excess of $25 million were between $250,000 and $1 million in 2021.
2 Merriam-Webster's dictionary defines "on spec" as: without having a definite buyer or customer but with the hope or expectation of finding one when work is completed.
3 *The Biz* does a great job explaining the legal side of production and financing, and I highly recommend it.
4 Here's the math, if you're interested. Let's assume that the distributor paid a minimum guarantee of $48,000 and is required to pay 60% of revenues

to the film's producers. (For simplicity, I'm ignoring the distributor's fees and expenses.) If the film generates $80,000 of revenue in its first week in theaters, then the distributor is supposed to pay 60% of $80,000, or $48,000 to the producers. However, they already paid a minimum guarantee of $48,000, so they don't have to pay any more. If the film produces revenues of $30,000 the next week, then the distributor has to remit 60% of it, or $18,000, to the producers. Of course, the producers are required to split the $18,000 amongst the investors and profit participants as required in their contracts.

Part 2
Financing Your Film

9 First Law of Film Finance

> If you're not making money for your investors, you're not making movies.
>
> – Jon Keeyes, producer

In the chapters to come, I will talk about three important numbers that define your movie: the budget, the financing plan, and the market value. Briefly, the budget is how much you plan to spend to make the entire movie, including development (if still needed), preproduction, production, and post-production. The financing plan is how you expect to raise the money needed to make the film, whether that is from equity, presales, soft money, or elsewhere. The market value of your movie is how much revenue you can reasonably expect it to earn once it is complete. This chapter shows how the budget, financing plan, and market value are connected.

These three numbers are tied together in a very important way. It must be the case that the market value is bigger than the financing plan. Remember, your equity investor is expecting to earn a 20% premium on their money. If the market value is $1 million and the financing plan is $1 million, then you will not have any extra money to pay that 20% premium. Even worse, you will not have money to pay yourself your back-end. Using the old elementary school math symbol for "greater than," > , we can say that:

Market Value > Financing Plan

This is one important rule for film finance that shows how these two numbers are tied together.

This relationship is tricky because the market value is not a firm number. There are so many unknowns before production has begun and one-to-two years before your film's releases. For instance, you do not know for certain who your stars will be, or if your genre will be popular by the time of release, or if a massive snow storm on the East Coast will knock out theaters on your opening weekend. Producer Stu Pollard reminds us that "you can't control how many people see your movie." The market value of your film is the best guess of (hopefully) experienced professionals. Developing an estimate of the market value will be covered in Chapter 10.

Nonetheless, this is finance, where we are trying our best to predict the future. If you did your work to estimate the market value of your film with the help of industry experts, then it is up to your financiers to take the leap of faith and hope it works out. But as long as your market value is bigger than your financing plan, there is a reasonable chance of a good outcome for your equity investors.

The only person who can tell you how much bigger the market value needs to be than the financing plan is your equity investor. If they are willing to invest, then the difference is big enough. If they are not willing to invest, then the difference is not big enough. *The Birthday Cake* producer Siena Oberman aims for her financing plan to be 60% of the market value of her films. She likes to present her potential equity investors with a "worst-case scenario," so that they can feel comfortable with their risks in a given film.

Now that the financing plan and market value are covered, we can build the budget in as well.

In order to pay all of the costs of making your film, you must raise enough cash from investors. In other words, your budget must equal your financing plan, at a bare minimum.[1] This mirrors the words of *American Psycho* producer Jeff Sackman, who repeats over and over for any filmmaker who will listen, "the budget and finance plan have to match." In practice, you will almost certainly need to raise more than your budget to get your movie made. For instance, if your production requires a completion bond, then you will need 10% more than your budget, as contingency to be set aside in case of emergencies. If you think you need $1 million to make the movie, your completion bonder may require you to have $1.1 million on hand.

Using the same chomping alligator mouth from before, we can say:

Financing Plan > Budget

One producer I spoke to worked for several years as a line producer, building budgets and thoroughly learning where costs lie in making films. They told me that they always add a little extra into their budgets, so they can show investors a bigger projected cost to allow them to raise a little extra money. For instance, if a particular special effect was expected to cost $50,000, they might show it costing $55,000 in the budget, in case extra labor was needed to manage it. In their mind, they were "padding the budget" and they "could get away with it" because they had credibility as a line producer.

I see this effort to add a safety cushion to the budget in a positive light. This is what smart financial managers do at companies and organizations all over the world – they build conservative budgets that allow the institution to carry on even in the case of a massive product recall, recession, or global pandemic. As an example, Habitat for Humanity is required to budget for a profit of $0 in order to maintain its nonprofit status. They clearly budget conservatively, because their income statements show actual profits of about $139 million in 2022 and $61 million in 2021.[2] The profit of $0 is what they expect to earn at the beginning of the year, and the $139 million result is what actually happened because of generous donations. Even though they are not supposed to earn a profit, they do because their revenue always comes in higher than expected or their costs come in lower than budgeted (or both).

I will not suggest that you misrepresent your expected costs to a potential investor, but I do think that building a budget that allows for the film to get finished even if bad things happen is just smart financial planning. Producer Clay Pecorin will tell you that "you always need to have money to fix a problem, because you're always going to have one." I also would encourage you to discuss the cushion that is built into your budget with your investors, so that they know you are making a prudent plan and they are on the same page as you.

All Together Now

Here is where things get really exciting! We already said earlier that the market value had to be bigger than the financing plan. We just figured out that the financing plan has to be bigger than the budget. Putting those two arguments all together reveals one of the most important takeaways of this entire book, the First Law of Film Finance:

> Market Value > Financing Plan > Budget

Behold the truth of film finance! Look upon it in its simplicity and obviousness! Wonder "why didn't someone write that into a book sooner?" If your market value is bigger than your financing plan, and if your financing plan is bigger than your budget, then your film is very likely to be a financial success, your investors are very likely to get repaid, and you are almost certainly going to be able to make several more films with great partners in the future.

This is not some hypothetical concept either. Many of the producers that I spoke to articulated the importance of this law to their career success. Over and over in my interviews, people told me the importance of the market value being bigger than the budget, or the budget being smaller than the financing plan. This law is the foundation of their businesses, and is the reason that they enjoyed the successes that they have experienced. For anyone who wants to make a career out of producing films, this relationship between market value, financing plan, and budget should drive all of their decisions.

This First Law of Film Finance also stresses that the most important financial metric of your film is, surprisingly, not the budget. It is the market value. If you do not know the market value of your film, then you cannot possibly know how to budget it. Producer Jeff Sackman noted that "the budget and financing plan don't always match the market value at the initiation of the film, and thus the billions of dollars that have been lost in independent film over the years." You can avoid being in the pool of producers who contributed to those billions of dollars of losses by following the First Law.

In the chapters that follow, I will explain more about how to use this law to build your business plan, raise money for your film, and complete it successfully.

Takeaways

- The First Law of Film Finance says that: Market Value > Financing Plan > Budget.
- Movies can only be financially successful if they follow this rule.

Notes

1 Producers use a wide variety of budget terms, including all-in budget, direct budget, final budget, final all-in budget, gross budget, ingoing budget, ingoing direct production budget, net budget, and shooting production budget. There does not seem to be consistency amongst those definitions, so always clarify with your partners. For the purposes of the First Law, I am defining budget to mean the costs of making the movie, all the way through post-production, but excluding the contingency, deposits, financing costs, and interest.
2 Sourced from the Consolidated Financial Statements and Report of Independent Certified Public Accountants for Habitat for Humanity International, Inc., Years ended June 30, 2022 and 2021 at https://www.habitat.org/media/12866/download

10 The Market Value of Your Film

> If you don't know the value of your project, then you can't get it made.
> – Stuart Pollok, producer

> Know the value of the film.
> – Nick Spicer, producer

Your unmade film has a market value.

How can it possibly have a market value before it is made? Your project is a tremendous work of art, the amazing culmination of years of sweat and hustle. It might even change the world. And it already has a market value before you shoot a single frame.

We already established in Chapter 2 that art has monetary value, and your film does too. In this chapter, I will explain how producers estimate the market value of their films before they are ever made.

Remember, the First Law of Film Finance says that:

Market Value > Financing Plan > Budget

To clarify, when producers use the term "market value," they typically mean how much revenue the film will generate via its first set of distribution contracts. In the simplest case, if a streaming service buys the worldwide distribution rights for ten years for $20 million, then the market value of the film is $20 million. The contract may be structured so that the producers are paid $2 million per year for the next ten years, but the market value would still be $20 million. (For those who know something about the time value of money, it is ignored in this definition of the market value.)

In a more traditional, windowed release, the film may first run in theaters, then shift to rentals, then move to a streaming or pay TV service, and then move to free TV. In this case, the market value is the sum of the revenue from all of these different distribution windows.

You may also hear people refer to the market value as the "ultimates" or "ultimate revenue." All three mean the same thing. (This is finance, where synonyms seem to exist just to confuse you.) The First Law of Film Finance could easily say that the ultimates must be bigger than the financing plan. I chose to use the phrase market value instead, because that was the term most commonly used by the producers that I interviewed.

The expected amount of tax incentives is also included in the definition of market value. On the income statement, tax incentives will show up as revenue, and the United States federal government will tax profits from them just like all other profits. Therefore, market value is estimated as:

Market Value = Value (Domestic + International Rights) + Tax Incentives + Ancillary Revenue

As you can tell from the First Law of Film Finance, the market value of the film is essential to your greenlighting process. If you cannot produce it at a budget below the market value, then your movie is probably not viable. Estimating the market value is hard work for early-career producers, and particularly so because there are no easy calculators, datasets, or off-the-shelf tools that you can use to estimate it. It will likely take you a lot of time, but it is critical to successfully finding investors for your film.

The market value of your film is also difficult to determine because it is in the future, not the present. A lot can change between when you begin principal photography and when you release the film. Your lead actor may have a break-out hit, your topic may suddenly be trending on Twitter, and your first-time director may create a masterpiece. An estimate of your film's value today may miss all of those factors.

However, you will want to present your potential investor with a plausible estimate of the market value of your film in order to gain their commitment. Going back to our discussion in Chapter 3, a viable estimate of the market value is incredibly helpful to making your investor comfortable making that leap of faith. Your goal is not to get the number right. Your goal is to generate a market value estimate that is backed by facts and analysis that is credible to your investor.

The burden is on you to make your potential investor feel confident in your estimate of the market value of your film. If they believe in your estimate, you are on the right path to gain their investment. If they do not believe your estimate, then you stand very little chance of winning their partnership.

Please notice that I use the phrase "estimate of the market value" a lot in this book. The true market value can only be known in the future, once the film is completed, sold, and distributed. Given that you are trying to raise money in the present, not the future, you cannot know the market value. You can only estimate it.

This chapter reviews five different ways that independent producers estimate the market values of their projects: $0 assumption, narrow comps, broad comps, sales estimates, and producer estimates. As you will see, none are perfect, although some are much better than others. The highs and lows of each are described below. I will start with the simplest, and then get more complicated. In the end, I hope that you will understand how to find the value of your film, so you know how much to budget to complete it and how much to raise from investors to get it made.

$0 Assumption

The simplest method to estimate the market value of your project is to presume it has no market value. From a legal perspective, that is the safest approach. Many lawsuits begin with a producer telling their potential investors their true estimated market value of the film. The investors commit, the film gets made, but then never finds distribution. The market value ends up being zero, and the investors sue the producers for misrepresenting the market value. You can avoid that lawsuit if you start your process assuming your film is worth $0.

If that is the case, then it affects all of your choices and how you approach your investors. To align with the First Law of Film Finance, your budget has to be as close to $0 as possible, as does your financing plan. Tax incentives are irrelevant, because the minimum required spend will not be reached. Your investors will still have a 120 and 50 position in your film, but knowing that there is almost no chance they will ever be paid anything. This route is essentially a bet that the film will be successful in the future, though since its estimated market value is $0, there is little recourse for investors if it never makes money. In other words, these people better like you a lot.

Pros

Beginning with the assumption that your film, like most other films, has no market value is very safe from a legal perspective. Attorneys will tell you that the market value of most films is $0, and claiming any market value other than $0 is going to result in you being sued for defrauding your investors. This method definitely minimizes your legal risk, and many lawyers reading this chapter would suggest that you just use this approach to estimating the market value of your film and move on to the next chapter.[1]

Even with a $0 market value assumption, you may still be able to find equity investors. They will need to be people who really believe in you (or really love you) and believe in your story.

Cons

However, assuming a $0 market value may also minimize the chances of your film ever getting made. With no market value, investors will not be clamoring to throw money on your dumpster fire. You could very easily fail in the other direction, in never making the movie at all.

If you are assuming your film has no market value, then your budget must be very close to $0 too. There is a history of films that accomplished this successfully, including *Paranormal Activity* (with a reported budget of $15,000), Independent Spirit Award winner *El Mariachi* ($7,000 budget), and Kevin Smith's *Clerks* (precisely $27,575). However, working with so little money in the production may also result in a finished movie that is so bad that it ruins your chances of producing again in the future.

On one hand, you need to arrive at an estimate of the market value so that you know how much you need to raise and how much you can spend. On the other hand, telling your investors that estimate to help make them comfortable with the amount of money that you are asking for could get you in legal hot water. This is yet another puzzle for all producers to solve. You need to weigh the legal risks against the other risks and figure out what makes you too uncomfortable to move on.

The $0 assumption approach to estimating the market value of your film is far from perfect. The good news is that there are other approaches that you might consider. The bad news is that they have their flaws too.

Narrow Comps

> The film business is difficult to comp, because it is an execution dependent business.
>
> – Ross Putman, producer & agent

Movies and private prisons have something in common.

You can let your imagination run wild with that statement to figure out just exactly what they have in common.

But I'll tell you. The value of both can be determined by comps.

Comps is short for comparable films, or comparable private prisons, or more generally, comparable transactions. Finance professionals use comps to find the market value of assets all the time. It is a well-established component of financial deal-making, from home buying to divorce settlements to multibillion dollar mergers and acquisitions.

For example, when the private prison operator CoreCivic acquired a facility from a developer in 2020, they could comp that prison against all of the other private prisons that they had recently acquired, and all of the ones their competitors had acquired too. The logic is simple. If these other similar prisons sold for $100 million each, then CoreCivic should not pay more than $100 million for this prison here.[2]

People estimate the market value of movies all the time using comps too. All. The. Time. Comps go into good business plans for independent films. Comps are also used by all of the major studios in their greenlighting decisions. There are good reasons to use comps to estimate the market value of your project.

In this section, I will focus on using a narrow set of films as comps. In the next section, I will explain the use of a broad set of comps.

Methodology

The producer selects a narrow group of films that are believed to be substantially similar to the project at hand. The number of comps selected is usually between three and five. It is at the producer's discretion to pick the exact films used as comps. The average box office performance of the comps is often used to estimate the value of the project.

Example

$147 million $268 million $115 million

Our Film's box office = $177 million!

Pros

Cherry-picking films like this gives a really high market value estimate for your project. That high value could translate to a higher budget and higher producer fees for you, if it were credible.

Cons

The use of a narrow set of comps comes with so many problems that make it a non-credible and unprofessional means of estimating the market value of your film. The problems begin with choosing the comps out of the hundreds of movies released every year. Selecting just a handful of comparable films suggests that there are only minimal differences between them and your film. In reality, there are meaningful differences, in the budget, casting, direction, major story themes, marketing, and so much more. Ignoring all of the other, similar films raises red flags.

The producer also has the incentive to pick the best-performing films when using narrow comps, so the estimates drawn from this methodology are biased upwards. Whatever you do, please do not include the biggest indie theatrical hits of all time in your comps. I cannot tell you how many times each year I hear someone tell a story about a new filmmaker who included either *Parasite*, *Paranormal Activity*, or *Get Out* in their comps, and then everyone in the room laughs knowingly. The story never ends with the filmmaker getting funding. Investors do not take these types of comps seriously because including them builds in the assumption that the film being pitched will be on par with the greatest filmmakers' masterpieces, and will also be lucky enough to be as financially successful. I've heard financiers describe these "black swan"-type of comps as dishonest, lazy, misleading, unhelpful, and unrealistic. You don't want any of those words to be associated with you. It is your job as the producer to be the reliable rock in the production, and your business plan needs to reflect you in that way.

It is also important to avoid picking older titles as your comps. The theatrical market changed dramatically in the past few years – even before COVID – and financial performance from more than five years ago is not representative of the current market. (No matter when you are reading this, I promise that the theatrical market has changed dramatically in the past five years.) As you are picking your comps, be sure to only use films from the very recent past, and definitely not more than five years old.

When producers cherry-pick narrow comps, they almost always share the box office receipts from the comps in the business plan, as in the example above. Unfortunately, box office is often the only publicly-available financial information that we have about a given film. Please remember that the box office is not the revenue on the film's income statement. The box office gets divided up amongst the distributor, the exhibitor, and the government, so only a portion of it appears as revenue on the film's income statement. The box office gives some indication of how much money a film will make in the downstream windows, like on streaming, free TV, and DVDs, but only people with access to proprietary information will know precisely how much. An estimate of box office from your comps is a crude tool in estimating the market value of a film.

These select masterpieces are anecdotes, not data. The potential investors that you will be meeting with are smart, savvy people who often make decisions based on data. *My Friend Dahmer* producer Milan Chakraborty will advise you that, "there's a certain deference you have to have and a respect for their business, and their business process." Your investors will appreciate a market value estimate drawn from a broad set of comps, and use it to make their decisions. Furthermore, if they are weighing an investment in you versus an investment in another producer, a credible estimate will give you an advantage.

Estimating your film's market value with a narrow set of comps is so much more dangerous than the $0 assumption. Narrow comps is the legally-riskiest of all methods presented in this chapter. It produces the most extreme estimates using the weakest methodology. Despite that fact, it is common practice in film business plans and pitch decks. I cannot recommend anyone ever estimate their film's market value with a set of narrow comps.

If you are estimating the market value of your film with comps, there is a much more professional and credible way to do it, which I describe in the next section.

Broad Comps

If you were preparing a comps analysis at a major studio, you would start with at least 30 movies that have several things in common with the proposed project. If you could find more than 30, that would be even better.[3] You would then run a complicated statistical analysis using all of the income statement data on each of those films over their lives to estimate the market value of the film. Even though almost none of that data is available to us outsiders, you can still learn from this methodology to improve upon your comps.

Methodology

When it comes to comps, more is better. By incorporating more titles into your set of comparable films, you are harnessing the power of data. You are no longer constrained to finding films that nearly perfectly match yours. Like a major studio, you should aim to have at least 30 movies in your comps. You will not always be able to find 30, for reasons I discuss below, but it is a reasonable goal.

Stowaway producer Nick Spicer advises you to "think about how realistic the comps are. Don't comp a Christopher Nolan movie or a Blumhouse massive success story. Comp things that are realistic targets." If your comps are realistic, then they will help persuade potential investors.

Finding perfect comps is impossible, because your film is the only one like it in the world. (If it isn't, you might want to move on to a different project.) You are looking for comps that are close enough. When I help filmmakers build their comps, I look for films that match the script across three or more themes. Imagine your film is a noir, female-led, minority-led, hospital-based, 1800s, war, romance, thriller starring Viola Davis. One of your comps may be a female-led, hospital-based romance. Another might be a Viola Davis war thriller. And that beloved noir American civil war film might be in there too. Once you are up to 30 movies, then all of the key themes from your script will be represented in your comps.

In the old days, we would use the box office from the comps to estimate the revenue that the film would generate. Now that so few movies get a theatrical release, sales prices are a better predictor. To estimate the market value of your film, find publicly-announced sales prices for comparable films. These are the prices that make the headlines coming out of Sundance, Cannes, or Toronto. For instance, on September 12, 2022, you could find stories all over about the sale of Alexander Payne's *The Holdovers* for $30 million. While the big deals are well publicized, most sales prices are harder to find. You will probably need to do some digging, as there is no central database of these announcements. Many sales are reported in the trades, especially IndieWire. Remember, your comps should all be from the last five years.

The average sales price for all of your comps is a good starting estimate for the market value of your film.[4]

Example

As an example, Table 10.1 shows a comps analysis for a script. This imaginary film features a minority, female lead, in a family drama/thriller about ambition in the music business. Information for 12 of the comps is shown in the table.

Table 10.1 Comparable Films

| This table shows feature films that are believed to be comparable to "Our Movie." All films in this database are non-sequel dramas. "Value" is the price that one or more distributors is believed to have paid for some of the rights to the film, as reported in the press in millions of US$, and can be assumed to be speculative. All films match "Our Movie" across at least three Story Themes. The themes used are as follows:
A: Female-driven   C: Ambition   E: Thriller
B: Minority-driven   D: Music   F: Family drama |

Film	Release	Value ($)	Buyer	A	B	C	D	E	F
Bad Hair	2020	8.0	Hulu	✓	✓	✓	✓		
Bruised	2020	20.0	Netflix	✓	✓	✓			✓
Cha Cha Real Smooth	2022	15.0	Apple	✓		✓	✓		✓
CODA	2021	25.0	Apple	✓		✓	✓		✓
Dual	2022	3.0	RLJE	✓		✓		✓	
Honk For Jesus. Save Your Soul.	2022	8.5	Focus	✓	✓	✓			✓
I Care a Lot	2021	10.0	Netflix	✓		✓		✓	
The Night House	2021	12.0	Searchlight	✓				✓	✓
Nanny	2022	7.0	Amazon	✓	✓	✓		✓	
Passing	2021	15.0	Netflix	✓	✓	✓			
Share	2019	2.0	A24	✓	✓			✓	
The Farewell	2019	6.0	A24	✓	✓				✓
⋮	⋮	⋮	⋮						
		18 more rows							
⋮	⋮	⋮	⋮						
		Average $11M							

	Market Value Scenarios				
Best case	Better case	Base case	Worse case	Worst case	
$11 million	$1.1 million	$550,000	$220,000	$0	

In addition to the year of release and the buyer, the market value of each film is presented. These values are the best available information about the sales of each film. For instance, Vulture reports that Searchlight acquired "worldwide distribution rights" for *Nanny* for $7 million, which is the market value shown in the table.[5] This is a really helpful estimate, because it is a specific dollar amount for global distribution. Less clearly, *IndieWire* stated that US-only rights to *Dual* were purchased by RLJE in a "low-mid seven figure deal for the film."[6] This is just domestic rights, not global, and a specific dollar amount is not given. At this point, you have the choice to either disregard this film in your comps, or make a reasonable assumption about the market value and include it. For the sake of creating a complete example, I chose to include *Dual* in these comps. I interpreted a low-mid seven figure deal to be somewhere between $2.5 million to $3.5 million. Taking the low end of the range, and adding an additional, safe assumption of $500,000 for international rights, gives my estimate of the market value of *Dual* at $3 million.

Dual is a female-driven thriller with themes of ambition. It is a reasonable comp for the script in this example, because it could be expected to attract the same audience. Each of the films in this set of comps has at least three themes in common with the proposed project, and some have more. The themes that I chose to build the comps are not necessarily the themes that you should use in your comps analysis. You will decide the important themes in your movie, and build a set of comps that match those themes. It is important that the themes are broad enough to find a large set of comps. If one of your themes is "protagonist eats lots of spaghetti straight from the pot while coloring a picture of a unicorn," then your comps table will be empty. Your goal is to find general themes that are likely to attract the same audience as your film.

There are six themes shown in the example, but that number is not set in stone either. You may find that you need to expand to eight or ten themes to build a large enough set of comps. The important thing is that each theme is a reason that your audience would go see the movie. Some people like female-driven family dramas about ambition, while others like minority-driven thrillers centered around music.

If your themes match a broad set of recent films, then that is a really good sign for your movie. It means that you are on track to make something that audiences will want to see, and that distributors are in the mood to buy.

In this example, there is a range of possible market value estimates for the film, from a $0 worst-case scenario to an $11 million best-case scenario. I will explain how I arrived at all five estimates, and the flex points around each.

The best-case scenario takes the simple average sales price of all of the films in the data, and assumes that the project does not earn tax incentives.[7] I consider the average to be the best-case scenario because these reported sales prices represent the top 1% of all independent films made. Just presenting a simple average is the equivalent of telling your investors that you expect your film to be in the top 1% of all independent movies.

The simple average from your broad comps is not a perfect way to solve for the market value of your film, because it has two big biases built in: a best-case scenario bias and a survivorship bias. The first bias comes from the fact that prices are announced or leaked for bigger purchases more often than they are for smaller purchases (i.e. Apple bought *Coda* for $25 million!). By using sales prices, you are biasing your market value upward by quite a bit because your comps are built using too many bigger sales and not enough smaller sales. Your resulting estimate is the very high end of the market value for your film, and a best-case scenario. That is only a problem if you do not recognize it, both for you and your investor. You certainly do not want to rush head-first into making your first movie based on a best-case market value. Neither your budget nor your financing plan should ever be based on the simple average sales price of your broad set of comps. You will probably never pay back your investors (if you ever find any), and have a much harder time raising funds for your next project.

The second problem with using sales prices to find market value is called a survivorship bias, which is a fancy way of saying that we can observe prices for movies that sell, but we can't observe prices for those that do not sell. Between these two biases, the problem arises that all of the low value and failed sales are going to be missing from your comps.

You want your investors to know that the market value derived from the simple average of the sales prices is a best-case scenario so that they are warned. An investor who is fully-informed about all of the risks of a project is less likely to sue than an investor who was only told about the best-case scenario. For that reason, you may want to include other scenarios, like those that you see at the bottom of Table 10.1.

The better-case scenario uses a quick math trick to scale back the simple average by dividing it by ten. The reason for dividing by ten is to simplify the uncertainty. There are so many possible outcomes for your film. It could sell for nothing, next to nothing, or a whole lot of money. We do not have data on all of those movies that sold for very little money, but there are definitely way more of them than the top 1% on this table. Dividing by 10 is the equivalent of assuming that for every one hit, there are nine misses.[8] It builds in the admittedly unrealistic assumption that either your project will sell like a top 1% film, or it will not sell at all. Those are the two ends of the spectrum, and ignore all of the possible outcomes in between, for the sake of simplifying the analysis. The unrealistic assumption is helpful in this case, to get to a more realistic estimate of the market value of the movie of $1.1 million.

This $1.1 million estimate is what is known in statistics as an expected value. It does not mean that your film is worth precisely $1.1 million. Instead, it is easier to think of as the outcome of making your movie many times. Imagine you could produce your film 10 times in 10 different universes. In each version, different talent is attached. The odds of making a hit are 1-in-10 in every universe. One version would work, but the other nine films would be flops (but not yours, Spider-Ham). Those 10 movies would be worth $1.1 million on average. In other words, your expected value is the average you would get if you could make your movie over and over.

Of course, you do not get to make your movie 10 times, so you will never see most of those outcomes. For your potential investor, that is irrelevant. If they are doing their job right, they will invest in your movie and many others. Diversifying across several projects gives them lots of chances to hit on a winner.

The base-case estimate of $550,000 uses the same math trick as the better case, but with a different underlying assumption. Instead of assuming a 1-in-10 chance of your film being a hit, it assumes 1-in-20. In other words, the estimate is calculated by dividing the best-case scenario estimate by 20. The choice of 1-in-20 in my analysis is equally as arbitrary as the choice of 1-in-10 used earlier, and is not grounded in any particular piece of information or statistic. At best, it serves to show the potential investor the outcome if the film is twice as risky as the better case suggests.

Of all of the estimates in this table, one could easily argue that the worse-case is the most accurate. The worse-case estimate of $220,000 assumes a poorer outcome for your film, just a 1-in-50 chance of being a hit. Those odds are roughly on par with your movie's likelihood of getting into the Sundance Film Festival, which often accepts 2% or less of submitted narrative features. The worse-case value in this example is calculated by simply dividing the best-case value by 50. Of course, you are welcome to tweak these odds in your analysis. They are not set in stone.

The $0 estimate is back as the worst-case scenario, to disclose to your potential investor the possibility that the film will have no value once it is completed. For legal cover and for the sake of being honest with your potential investors, I support showing $0 as a possible outcome. It happens. It has even happened to respectable studios, that threw out completed films (i.e. *Batgirl* at Warner Brothers[9]) because they were too messy, too controversial to release, or tied up in legal matters.

The market value of your film includes all revenue earned, including tax incentives. If you expect your film to collect a tax incentive, be sure to add it to all of these values too. For example, if the expected tax incentive for the project in Table 2 is $200,000, then the best case increases to $11.2 million, and the worst case changes to $200,000.

This range of estimates gives you a place to start a conversation with potential investors. It shows uncertainty, with the potential of a nice upside, and a difficult downside.

To reiterate, there are lots of decisions that you need to make to estimate a market value based on a broad set of comps. It is up to you to pick the themes to match against, to decide whether to include vague sales information like in the case of *Dual*, to decide how many market value scenarios to include and the odds for each. There are no right answers here. You will only know if you have done enough when you convince someone to invest in your film.

While the analysis above was conducted with a narrative film in mind, it would work just as well with documentaries. Plenty of docs sell at festivals and markets, and their sales prices are occasionally reported too.

Pros

More data provides more information. You would rather trust a survey that asked 25,000 voters about their preferred candidate than one that only asked five voters. Similarly, your potential investor is more likely to have faith in your estimate of the market value of your film using a broad set of comps instead of five narrow ones. There are very few cases in life in which less data is better.

The data is not perfect. In some cases, only the value of the North American rights might be publicized. In other cases, the price reported may be rumored, but not confirmed. If you have lots of films in your dataset, then the imperfections get diluted. They do not go away completely, but they get significantly reduced. This is another reason for having more films in your comps.

Using a broad set of comps is also less likely to land you in a legal mess than narrow comps, because the data gives you the ability to show a much broader range of potential outcomes. In the example, you can see five potential market values for the film, ranging from the $0 worst case scenario to the $11 million best-case scenario. These estimates do not pin you down to a specific number that you have to achieve in order to avoid being sued. Of course, you can still be sued for defrauding investors by using a broad set of comps, so tread cautiously. And this chapter is as much about helping you get your film made as it is helping you avoid getting sued.

Cons

One problem with using comps is actually finding sales prices that you can use. It seems that fewer sales prices have leaked in recent years, which makes a good comps analysis even more difficult. For full disclosure, I could not find 30 comps for my example for this chapter. I hope that is due to a shortage of films sold at festivals in 2020, but may be a trend going forward. While 30 films is the goal, the actual number that you need is just enough to make your investor comfortable. If you cannot reach that number, then you will need to use a different method described in this chapter to find the value of your film.

The broad comps in this table also ignore the value of the on-screen talent. While A-list stars no longer guarantee a certain level of box office at the theater, they do guarantee a certain level of viewership on streaming services.

Finding the market value of your movie using broad comps is not the perfect tool, but it is the best tool that many aspiring filmmakers have at their disposal.

Sales Estimates

> If you are able to put together sales estimates and a financing plan, then you can convince investors based on a model.
>
> – Siena Oberman, producer

Sales agents have a superpower: they can credibly estimate the market value of your film.

Sales agents are like walking, breathing film value calculators. They are amazing. And they can do this work in their head because they are constantly working to find distributors for their clients' films. Through the course of negotiating deals, sales agents see all of the data and all of the trends. They understand what sells well, with which stars, in which territories, on which platforms (including subscription video on demand and ad-supported video on demand). They also know which distributors still have money to spend in their budget this year, and which are tight on cash. Competent sales agents use all of this information, along with their confidential, inside knowledge of recent sales prices, to build sales estimates.

Legendary entertainment attorney Tom Ara will tell you that "the budget can't dictate the sales estimates. The market dictates the sales estimates." Sales estimates are projections of how much the movie will sell for in various territories when it is completed. They are primarily based on two key features of your film, the actors and the genre. That's what matters most to sales agents. Far less important to the sales estimate are factors like how good your surprise ending is, how amazing your cinematographer is, or anything else that makes your film a unique and wonderful work of art. What buyers know is that subscribers will click the "Play" button if your movie is of the right genre, and if the stars are big and recognizable.

Stars matter. One producer told me that, "Hollywood is full of actors walking around with dollar amounts on their heads." Especially in the world of streaming, having a thumbnail picture of a recognizable actor next to the film adds a lot of value. (I heard someone call this the new Rule of Thumb recently, and I wish I remember who so I could give them credit.) That value is driven by the picture of the star on the thumbnail image for the title. For instance, starting in 2020, Netflix was way more excited to show Anya Taylor-Joy in the thumbnail image for *Peaky Blinders* than the show's star, Cillian Murphy. Coming off the success of the limited series *The Queen's Gambit*, Ms. Taylor-Joy was more recognizable, especially to Netflix subscribers. Netflix switched out the images to drive more viewership of *Peaky Blinders*, and it apparently worked. If you can get an actor with a $2 million sign stuck to their head, you can expect to sell your film for at least $2 million. Of course, such signs do not literally exist, and different sales agents may attach different dollar amounts to certain talent, but it is definitely true that some actors bring more sales to their films than others.

If you do not have a good understanding of how to attach talent to your film, the bad news is that there is no book or class in the world that can teach you how to do it. You really have two choices. Your first option is to go to work for a company where you are either representing talent or hiring talent. Spend a few years and learn the ropes from a talent agency, production company, or casting director, as so many other successful producers have done. The second option is to find a producer who knows how to attach talent, and convince them to work with you on your films. Of course, with enough money, you can cast the biggest stars to your film and ignore the two options I offered.

The genres that work in the presales market vary little over time. Action, horror, thriller, and dog movies sell well most years. Comedies, dramas, and rom-coms do not (comedy does not translate well, and drama is really dependent on the director's execution of the script). Listen to the panels with sales agents at film events like the American Film Market to get the latest on what is and isn't selling.

Methodology

If you have a budget over $1 million and at least one recognizable star attached, you should be able to find a reputable sales agent to give you estimates for the prices that you will get for your film in various territories around the world. Your sales agent may conclude that your film will fetch a decent price in Japan, Latin America, and the UK. Add up the values from all of the territories, add in the value of your tax incentives, and you have an estimate of the market value of your film.

The best way to meet sales agents is by going to one of the big four film markets: the European Film Market, Cannes, Toronto, and the American Film Market (AFM). You will need to pay for a badge to get access to the market and the directory of attendees. There is a bit of sticker shock with badge prices, recently costing hundreds of dollars for in-person attendance. Plan ahead, and schedule meetings with sales agents who recently represented films like yours. If you show up at the market prepared, you stand a good chance of finding a sales agent who will help you estimate the market value of your film (and more). You will get your money's worth.

At AFM, the entire Loews Santa Monica Beach Hotel is converted to an office building. The beds are removed from each hotel room, and moved off-site for the week. Sales agents and distributors move in office furniture, big screens, and marketing materials, to make the room feel professional (never mind that there is still a hotel bathroom right at the entry of each room). In that environment, meeting a ton of people is really easy, because it is just a matter of moving from one hotel room to the next (but preferably by appointment).

I love the energy in the hallways at AFM. They are always crowded, and often filled with young, nervous, uncertain producers. You will fit right in!

You can certainly try meeting with sales agents in person or on video calls outside of the markets too. It will be a harder slog to find them without the film market's directory, but use your network to make connections. It is worth noting that the talent agencies, like CAA, WME, and their peers have divisions that also behave as sales agents, and can also provide sales estimates. You may find that they are harder to meet than the traditional sales agents at the film markets.

Of course, the sales estimates that you got before preproduction began will probably be wrong by the time your movie is released. Sales agents are pretty close to getting the sales estimates right on average, but can miss quite substantially on any given picture. This is not their fault – they are trying to make their best estimate with the information that they have today, just like you. So long as your financiers understand that the sales estimates are not revenue guarantees, then you are less likely to be sued.

Sales estimates change over time for a lot of reasons. First, the market for finished films is in constant flux, with new distribution technologies coming in, and older technologies fading out. Second, actors' values are not stagnant. Some rise as they gain bigger and better roles and awards, while others fade as they age or get caught in a scandal (right, Kevin Spacey?). Third, the themes that audiences want to see change as social moods change. Consider the films nominated at the Oscars and other awards shows somewhat of a reflection of the national and international consciousness in a given year.

Cherry producer Judd Payne told me that they made the movie with a budget higher than the early sales estimates of $10 million, because they believed in the directors, the Russo brothers, and "their passion for the story." Oh boy, were they right! Apple reportedly bought the film for about $40 million, four times more than the sales estimates projected. Arguably, Judd Payne and his partner Matthew Rhodes at The Hideaway were able to take the risk on *Cherry* because they had years of experience and credibility. They believed that the film was worth more than $10 million, and luckily were proven right.

In my interviews with producers for this book, quite a few admitted to knowingly violating the First Law of Film Finance for one particular film, in far worse ways than Mr. Payne and Mr. Rhodes did. One of the panelists at a recent American Film Market finance conference even blatantly encouraged new producers to ignore the relationship between market value and budget. All of these rule-breakers have one thing in common: they already built their career and are in a good place to take big risks. A huge miss is not going to ruin their reputation amongst the creative community. A large loss is not going to chase away their investors either. These are the folks who have earned the right to take a big chance.

People at the early end of their producing career are not similarly situated. A producer who has a huge miss on their first film may never get another shot. For early-career producers, I would never encourage spending more to make a film than the early estimates of its market value. If your first film is viewed as financially irresponsible, it will be much harder to make a second film. The industry doesn't work like an episode of *Entourage* where a disregard for the system's safety rails is constantly rewarded.

* * *

Once you have sales estimates in hand, the next decision that you need to make is what to do with them. If you are happy with the estimates, and they establish a market value for your film that is higher than the financing plan, then you can ask your sales agent to begin the presales process. If all goes well, you will line up minimum guarantees from distributors and start production in no time.

You can get a loan backed by your minimum guarantees, but you do not have to. Siena Oberman followed a different strategy with *Birthday Cake* and other films. Once she knows that her project complies with the first law, she begins approaching equity investors to finance the entire movie. Her goal is to avoid splitting financiers into a safer group (lenders) and a riskier group (equity investors). Ms. Oberman prefers for her equity investors to roll the safer bet into their deal, rather than letting lenders take the easy money off the table.

The only obvious downside to the strategy of not using lenders is that you need to find equity investors who can contribute a lot more money. That may not be as challenging as it sounds. If the equity investors know that their investment is safer, then they may be willing to fund substantially more of the budget. Ultimately, you and your equity investors will have to decide the best way to structure the deal for both parties.

Pros

Sales estimates are the most credible of the five ways to estimate market value that are presented in this chapter. They are based on lots of good, proprietary data, coming straight from professionals who participate in the market regularly. In general, they are not biased like comps can be, because the sales agent has strong incentives to be accurate. They do not want to waste their time selling films with little or no value, but do want to generate as much revenue as possible for the films that they choose to sell.

Sales estimates also do not rely on you to do the work. While someday you might be skilled at estimating the market value of a film, you probably are not there yet. Instead of putting the burden on you, you can shift the burden to a sales agent.

Cons

While sales estimates from good agents are free, their big downside is that they are hard to get on your first film. Sales agents like to see a track record, big stars, and a reasonably large budget. If you cannot bring all three to the table, then you may not be able to gain estimates from a reputable sales agency. But never say never. If you begin getting to know sales agents now, then the worst that can happen is that you will have connections when you have a future project that they will want to represent. Networking now is an investment in your future career.

The market for presales is also shrinking quickly, as discussed in Chapter 4. With fewer projects selling, there is less data than in recent years on market values. Both the shifts in the presales market and the shortage of data mean that sales estimates may be less accurate and harder to get now than in the past.

Producer Estimates

> Find a producer who gives you credibility with financiers and talent.
> – Janet Yang, producer & president of the
> Academy of Motion Picture Arts and Sciences

If all of this sounds a bit too difficult, there is another, costlier route to generating a market value estimate for your film: bring on-board a very seasoned producer. Like a sales agent, a producer with lots of films under their belt also knows the market value of a lot of films. They know how much their own films sold for (or didn't sell for), and also know how much their friends' films sold for, and probably have an intern who used to work at a sales agency and shared some of those prices too. If you choose to partner with an experienced producer who can credibly estimate the market value of your film, then your problem is solved.

This should also serve as a hint on how you can sustain your own career. If you are good at estimating the market values of films and investors trust you, then you are likely to have a long, happy producing career and make lots of shows. This is a terrific skillset to develop, and I wish you the best of luck in crafting it.

Methodology

Build and use your professional network to find an experienced producer who likes you, likes your script, and wants to help. No doubt, the hard part here will be getting the producer on board. Producers with the ability to estimate the market value of a film also probably know a lot of investors, so their services are in demand. The hungriest can and will get their foot in the door. Like sales agents, the easiest place to meet them is at film markets and festivals. Begin building those relationships as soon as possible, so that you have time to find the right person who you would be able to work with and who would be willing to work with you. (There is much more about this in Chapter 14.)

Pros

A market value estimate from a credible producer is likely to be more reliable than broad comps, narrow comps, or a $0 estimate. This also shifts the burden of creating the estimate from you to a producing partner, so you can focus on your strengths.

Cons

I mentioned that this route is costly. You will have to give this producer a share of the producing fees and the equity. You will also lose some control over the film. However, given the options of getting the film made that launches your career with a seasoned producer on board or not getting the film made at all, the better choice is obvious.

From a potential investor's perspective, market value estimates created by a producer working on the project may not be viewed as credibly as estimates from a sales agent. The producer is biased towards the movie and may be perceived as overestimating its value.

Prepare to Pivot

> If the value is less than the budget, then you have got to figure out a way around that.
>
> – Nick Spicer, producer

If your market value is lower than the preliminary budget, then you need to pivot. To make your project viable, either lower the budget, raise the market value, or find soft money to make up the gap. Work with a great line producer to get the budget as low as possible. Also talk with your sales agent or experienced producers about how you could increase the market value of your film. Maybe different casting or tweaks to the story will help. Both the topics of budgeting and creating a commercially marketable package are beyond the scope of this book, but there are lots of other good books on those topics listed in the appendix.

The irony is not lost on me that one of the central principles of this book is that you must find a credible estimate for the market value of your film, and one of the central conflicts of this book is that finding a credible estimate of the market value of your film is very difficult and I cannot point you to off-the-shelf tools to help.

As a producer, you will spend your whole career resolving two key problems. The first is the catch-22 of attaching talent without financing, and attaching financing without talent. The second is properly estimating the market value of your film while it is still in development, usually without talent attached. Both problems become easier as you gain experience, but they never, ever go away. You will build a network of potential financiers as you produce more films, so it will be easier to find people to ask for money. You will build connections with talent, agents, and managers, so it will be easier to get your scripts in front of the right people. You will grow a network of sales agents who can help you determine the market value of your film, and you will also develop a better sense of what films are worth as you make more and more. The problems do not go away, but they get easier to manage.

Takeaways

- Determining the market value of your film is difficult but necessary work.
- There are five ways to estimate the market value, each with its pros and cons.

- If the market value of your project ends up lower than needed, then you need to pivot to make it work within the First Law of Film Finance.

Notes

1 *Grow House* producer William J. (Bill) MacDonald did not take a credit on most of his early films, because he was afraid of liability.
2 I totally realize that equating movies to private prisons is weird. I do not mean to imply that they are similar businesses at all, morally or otherwise.
3 The number 30 is a practical minimum. A studio greenlight team's statistical analysis probably would not work with less than 30 films.
4 Microsoft Excel or Google Sheets can solve for the average for you just by using the =average formula. Many YouTube videos can show you how to do that in under a minute.
5 https://www.vulture.com/2020/02/sundance-2020-a-complete-list-of-movies-sold.html
6 https://deadline.com/2022/01/dual-rlje-film-acquire-karen-gillan-sundance-sci-fi-thriller-1234919545/
7 I assume $0 of tax incentives to make this section simpler. If there was a tax incentive, it would just be added on to all of these values. For instance, a $100,000 tax incentive would make the best-case value $11.1 million and the worst-case value $100,000.
8 Technically, it is a weighted average, giving lots of weight to the possibility of a miss and a little weight to the possibility of a hit.
9 See: https://www.cnn.com/2022/08/03/entertainment/batgirl-movie-not-releasing/index.html

11 A Financing Plan

> Don't spend any money until it's fully financed.
> – Matt Manjourides, producer

The First Law of Film Finance says that:

Market Value > Financing Plan > Budget

The previous chapter provided strategies and methodologies to establish the market value of your film, and this chapter will give you guidance on your financing plan.

As you are building the broader business plan for your film, the financing plan is one key part of it. It does not need to be a separate document. Finance is just one part of your movie's business, which also includes the hiring, production, marketing, and distribution. (In other words, I would not use the terms "financing plan" and "business plan" interchangeably.)

The audience for your financing plan is all of your potential financiers. Anyone who puts money into your film wants to know where the rest of the money will come from. They certainly do not want to give you a chunk of cash, only to find that you have no idea how to raise the rest. Equity investors want to know how easy it will be to gather the remainder of the money needed. Lenders want to know how much equity you will require, and where it will come from. Even talent will want to see a meaningful finance plan to help them estimate the likelihood that your film will get made.

The best way to think of your financing plan is as a pie. Let's imagine that you need $500,000 to make your movie. Where will it come from?

As an example, maybe your financing plan looks like this pie chart in Figure 11.1. You have already put in $25,000 of your own money, or 5% of the plan. You expect 20% of your needs to be met by a loan against your presales minimum guarantees. Your lender will give you another 5% as a gap loan, backed by unsold territories. Another 10%

Figure 11.1 Financing Plan = $500,000

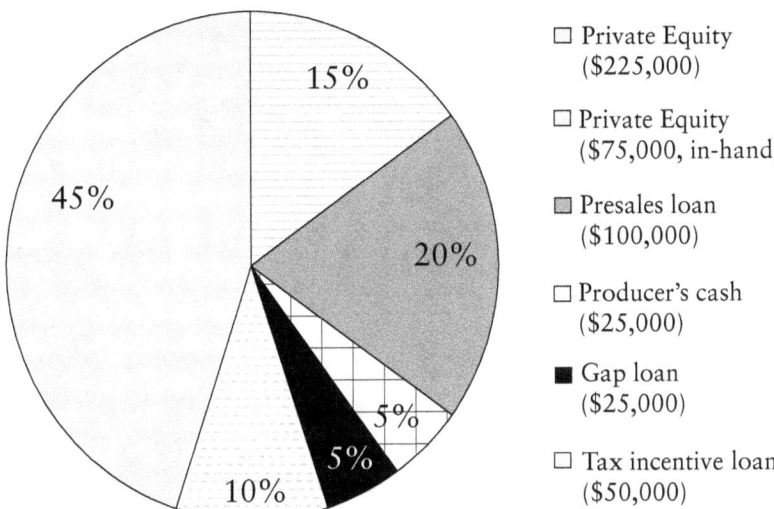

- Private Equity ($225,000)
- Private Equity ($75,000, in-hand)
- Presales loan ($100,000)
- Producer's cash ($25,000)
- Gap loan ($25,000)
- Tax incentive loan ($50,000)

This figure shows an example of the sources of cash that could make up a financing plan for a film, and the proportion of the financing plan that each source represents.

can be funded by tax incentives. If you already raised 15% of the plan through private equity (thanks Gramma!), then that leaves $225,000, or 45%, that needs to come from another private investor.

This example shows that, in order to build a financing plan, you need to do a lot of work ahead of time. In this set-up, you need to work with a sales agent or experienced producer to generate estimates of how well your film will sell. You need to work with a tax incentive consultant and lender to determine where to shoot and how much of a tax incentive you are likely to collect. Of course, you also need to work with a line producer to figure out a workable budget. In other words, producers ideally figure out the market value of their film first, then estimate the budget, and then build a financing plan.

Like a budget, a financing plan is a best guess. It is your plan for how the financing of your movie will come together, but it is not the end result. Between the moment that you first put your financing plan together, and the moment when all of the funds are in the bank, a lot will change. Your budget may go up. Your sales agent may find another buyer. Your shooting location and tax incentive may change. Your dear, sweet, foul-mouthed Gramma may give you more money.

You should continually update the financing plan in your broader business plan to reflect the changing financial realities of your film. (If you are hiring a graphic designer to make your business plan look

Financing Your Film

Figure 11.2 Sample Comparison of Market Value & Financing Plan

This figure shows an example of the relative size of a film's financing plan to its market value. In this case, the market value is the sum of presales, tax credits, and unsold rights. The financing plan is the sum of presale loans, tax credit loans, and equity.

good, maybe negotiate for a certain number of minor revisions to be included in the price.)

Joel Shapiro, producer of *Dear Dictator*, has specific targets that he tries to hit with his financing plan, as depicted in Figure 11.2. He aims for the loans based off tax credits and foreign sales to make up two-thirds of his financing plan. The remaining one-third then needs to be financed by an equity investor. Presumably, the equity will be repaid by the yet-to-be-sold domestic and foreign distribution rights, the value of which is estimated by a sales agent. To entice and protect that investor, Mr. Shapiro also tries to make sure that the market value of the unsold rights is double the amount of the needed equity investment. This second target is critical to his success in raising money for his films. He told me that, "even if the sales companies' estimates were wrong by 50%, the investors should still be made whole." His track record shows that Mr. Shapiro is able to find equity investors who are willing to take the risk with the market value of unsold rights worth double the amount of equity in the financing plan.

Mitigate the Risk

You probably know Peter Billingsley as the child actor who played the iconic Ralphie in the holiday classic, *A Christmas Story*. You may be surprised to hear the phrase that Mr. Billingsley repeated over and over when I spoke to him for this book: "Mitigate the risk."

Mr. Billingsley is now a successful producer, earning an Executive Producer credit on the movie that saved Marvel, *Iron Man*. He has narratives, documentaries, and television series under his belt, and a wealth of experience producing both inside and outside of the studio system.

So when Mr. Billingsley says, "mitigate the risk," I hope you will trust that they are wise words. Equity investors clearly stomach a lot of risk. It is your job as the producer to reduce that risk. You have a duty to get the equity piece of the financing plan as small as possible, and improve the odds of the film being financially successful to the best of your ability. Your finance plan should spell out how you will mitigate the risk for your investors.

Producers told me about lots of different risk mitigation devices they use, including but not limited to:

1. Lining up distribution before production begins.
2. Using tax incentives, grants, and other sources of soft money to help complete the budget.
3. Attaching marketable talent to improve the chances of a sale to domestic and foreign distributors.
4. Using loans against presales contracts to add cash to complete the budget.
5. Hiring top-notch line producers and production accountants to ensure that the budget is reasonable and the cash-on-hand is protected from theft, fraud, and embezzlement.
6. Minimizing the budget, to ensure that there is as much upside as possible for the equity investors.
7. Shooting beyond the reach of the labor unions or contracting early with them, to reduce the risk of work stoppages.[1]
8. Using deferrals to reduce the budget.
9. Contracting with a collection account manager to properly distribute revenue to investors and profit participants in the waterfall.
10. Not using real guns on set.
11. Locking foreign currencies with the help of a foreign exchange (FX) advisor to ensure that shifts in exchange rates do not leave the production short on cash.
12. Using insurance and completion bonds to protect the film.

When your potential equity investor asks, "How are you going to mitigate my risk?" you should already have a list of devices like this ready to share as part of your financing plan.

A Waterfall

The outcome of your completed financing is a waterfall, and it determines who gets paid in priority. The legal term, priority, is important, because parties with more priority are higher up in the waterfall, and parties with less priority are lower down in the waterfall. For all of your investors, the waterfall is the key, because it tells them how likely they are to get repaid on their contribution to your financing plan as revenue comes in. In your negotiations with lenders, equity investors, and talent, you will need to be very careful about giving away positions in the waterfall.

A sample waterfall is shown in Table 11.1 below. You might want to bookmark, screenshot, or copy this, because you will want to be able to flip back to it quickly.

The waterfall begins with an assumption about the market value of the film. I calculate the market value like in Chapter 10, as the revenue that the film is projected to generate, including the tax incentives that it should receive. I will begin with the unrealistic assumption that the market value is the same as the value of the financing plan at $500,000.

It is important to note that cash comes into the waterfall from your distributors and from the government providing your tax incentive. That means that theater owners have already taken their share out of the box office (typically keeping about 50% domestically and closer to 75% in international markets), and the distributors have already taken their share too. All revenue from other sources, such as DVD revenue, pay TV contracts, and toy licensing deals flows into the top of the waterfall too.

The waterfall is loosely divided into three sections, based on the balance sheet and income statement that we talked about in Chapter 3. The top of the waterfall pays out unpaid expenses on the income statement. The middle of the waterfall allows the debts on the balance sheet to recoup. The bottom section is where equity investors and participants finally begin to see their share of profits.

The collection account manager often pays themselves first in the waterfall. They are usually in priority position #1. They have the power to say that they will not manage collections on your film unless they are paid a share of the revenues. That power comes from the investors, who insist on a good, impartial collection account manager to protect their interests. There are two firms that dominate the market, Fintage House and Freeway. Your investor will almost certainly insist that one of the two run the collection account, and both will only manage your collections if they are assured to be paid for doing the work. I promise that having an independent collection account manager paying the right people in the waterfall in the correct order makes your life easier, and is well worth the money.

Table 11.1 Waterfall Example

This table shows all of the parties who are to be repaid by the revenue earned by the film. They are listed in order of priority, indicating which party is paid before others. Two scenarios are presented, showing the payments that result from different market values of the film. The financing plan represents the amount of cash each party contributed.

Priority position	Party	Amount repaid		Financing Plan
		Scenario 1	Scenario 2	
	Market Value (Revenue incl. tax credits)	$500,000	$1,000,000	
	Expenses			
1	CAM fee (1%)	$5,000	$10,000	
2	Guilds (6%)	$30,000	$60,000	
3	Sales agent (7%)	$35,000	$70,000	
	Total Expenses	$70,000	$140,000	
	Remaining balance to be distributed (Market value - Total expenses)	$430,000	$860,000	
	Liabilities			
4	Presales Loans (incl. interest and fees)	$135,000	$135,000	$100,000
5	Tax Credit Loan (incl. interest and fees)	$65,000	$65,000	$50,000
6	Gap Loan (incl. interest and fees)	$38,000	$38,000	$25,000
7	Equity recoupment + 20%	$192,000	$270,000	$225,000
8	Gramma recoupment + 20%	$0	$90,000	$75,000
9	Producer's cash	$0	$25,000	$25,000
10	Actor #1 deferral	$0	$60,000	
11	Actor #2 deferral	$0	$30,000	
12	Producer's cash 10% premium	$0	$2,500	
13	Producer fees	$0	$70,000	
	Total Liabilities	$430,000	$785,500	$500,000
	Remaining balance to be distributed (Prior Balance - Total liabilities)	$0	$74,500	
	Equity (50% of profits)			
14	Gramma (1/4 of equity)	$0	$9,313	
14	Equity Investor (3/4 of equity)	$0	$27,938	
	Participants (50% of profits)			
14	Director (6 points)	$0	$4,470	
14	Actor #1 (15 points)	$0	$11,175	
14	Actor #2 (7 points)	$0	$5,215	
14	Writer (2 points)	$0	$1,490	
14	Producer (20 points)	$0	$14,900	
	Remaining balance (Prior Balance - Total participations)	$0	$0	

In this example, I assumed that the collection account manager would take 1% of revenues off the top, but that number is not set in stone. While they are usually priority #1, that is not predetermined either. On a big film with a reputable bank as a lender, the collection account manager may defer their fee until after the bank is repaid in full. This very first line is a nice reminder that everything in the waterfall is up to negotiation.

The unions often come next, in priority position #2. If any residuals or other payments are due, they get paid high up in the waterfall. Producers must remain off the unions' naughty lists if they want to make more movies, and paying on time helps. I used a 6% assumption for the residuals, but the actual rate your film pays to the guilds will depend on a lot of variables.[2]

The sales agents are usually in the top of the waterfall too. The contract that you sign with them will require you to pay your sales agent a percentage of the revenue generated by your film. This is a really good incentive structure, because your sales agent gets a big payoff if they sell your film well. It aligns their incentives with your goals. How much you pay them is up to negotiation. In my example, they are supposed to get 7% of all revenues, excluding the tax incentive.

Your sales agent is also the party who is responsible for collecting the money that you are owed from the distributors. For instance, if you are still owed money from three years ago by a pay TV channel in Brazil, your sales agent is the one who will work to get it for you. Again, they should have the incentive to collect because they are paid a percentage of whatever they can shake out of those folks who owe you money.[3] Former entertainment banker Lisa Wolofsky will tell you that "some sales agents are on top of their collections," implying that others are not. You may want to ask some tough questions about their collections process before signing with a sales agent.

If there are other bills that did not get paid out of the film's bank account yet, those might get settled here too. For instance, if you still owe some money for your postproduction work, then it should get paid in the top of the waterfall.

Pause here to look back at the waterfall in Table 11.1, to make sure you understand that first section and see what is coming.

What happens on the next few lines, as we reach the middle of the waterfall, is the real free-for-all. Once the income statement part is completed and the balance sheet part begins, anything goes. Don't get me wrong – this is not *The Purge* – there are contracts that need to be followed. However, the order of priority at this point is up to negotiation. The highest priority will belong to the entity with the most negotiating power (or the best attorneys).

There are potentially numerous parties that need to be repaid here. Any lenders will likely get higher priority. The senior lenders who loan you money based on a contract, such as a presales lender or tax credit lender, will insert themselves here, to ensure that any balances on their loans get paid. After all, the tax credit payment is supposed to cover the entire balance of the tax credit loan, but if it does not, the film still owes.

In this example, I show the presales loans in priority position #4 in the waterfall. Notice that the loans provides $100,000 to the financing plan, but it costs $135,000 to repay the loans. You will always have to repay more than you borrow because of interest and fees. The interest is the bank's motivation for lending to you. Just as we talked about in Chapter 3, all investors look for a return on their savings, and banks are the same. If they cannot generate a return by lending to you, then they will lend their savings to another borrower that will pay interest. The fees cover all of the banks costs for setting up the loans. You will actually pay for their lawyers in those fees. The bank will not lend to you without a completion bond in place for your film, and the cost of that bond is included in your loans too. The bank will pay the bonder for you, so that cost never shows up in your spending. You will want to work with a lender or sales agent to get estimates of how much you can borrow and how much you will need to repay.

When the film is released, your distributors' minimum guarantees are paid into your film's collection account. They are revenue for your film. Three possible outcomes can then hit the waterfall. If the minimum guarantees add up to $135,000, and it costs $135,000 to repay the loans, then you are done with that line on the waterfall. In a better outcome, the minimum guarantees pay more than the amount owed, and that extra cash can flow down the waterfall to the next position. In the worst of the three scenarios, your film is later than expected getting to your distributors, and the interest costs on your loans grow. In that case, there is a chance that your minimum guarantees will not cover the cost of the loans, and money is sucked up the waterfall to repay the bank first.

All of these notes in the past two paragraphs also apply to tax incentive loans. You will pay back more than you get for your budget from the tax incentive lender. If the government takes a long time processing your tax incentive or it takes you a long time to sell it, then you will owe more because interest will keep adding on every day. There will be fees tacked on as well. The only important difference is that the presales loan is expected to be repaid with minimum guarantees, while the tax incentive loan is normally repaid with the money generated by the tax incentive.

Gap and mezz lenders, which were discussed in Chapter 4, will also be in this part of the waterfall, hoping that those unsold territories finally sell and provide a return. It is almost always the case that the senior lenders' unpaid balances get a higher position in the waterfall than gap and mezz. In my example, I added a $25,000 gap loan in priority position #6, but no mezz. As with the other loans, the amount that needs to be repaid is more than the amount borrowed.

The 120 part of your equity investors' 120 and 50 will be in the middle of the waterfall too. The other piece, the 50% of profits, sits in the bottom section. I decided to assume that your Gramma would be nice, and allow the other equity investor to recoup their 120 before she recoups her 120. Chances are, your equity financiers will want to be paid pro rata and pari passu (i.e. at the same time and in proportion to how much they invested).

I also added a line in to repay the producers for $25,000 of their own cash that they spent in development and preproduction. If you want to similarly be repaid, keep receipts, contracts, a journal, and any other records you can of all of the money you spent early on in the film's life. Anyone you take out to lunch to talk about the movie, regardless of whether the meeting was fruitful or not, should be included in those records. All of this evidence will convince your investors that you should be treated as an investor too. You will need to negotiate with your investors whether you should get interest on this money as well. In this example, I added a 10% premium to your cash outlay, but presumed that you would only recoup it after your actors received their deferred compensation.

Any talent who took a deferral will also be somewhere in the middle of the waterfall. They may be all together, paid pro rata and pari passu, or they may be spread out as some negotiated better than others. If you deferred your producer's fee, it will likely be in this vicinity.[4]

The bottom of the waterfall is the real estate of the profit participants. If there is any money left, your participants and equity positions finally get paid. If all goes well, you get paid there too.

It is possible but unlikely that you will have a profit participant much higher up in the waterfall. For instance, earlier I mentioned that Sandra Bullock's participation contract on *Gravity* reportedly paid her over $70 million. Called a "first dollar gross" participation deal, it gave her a cut of all revenue, above the lender (in that case, Warner Bros.) and all other participants in the waterfall. Chances are, if you sign a contract like that with a big star, then you will not be able to find an equity investor. Equity positions are already risky enough without being buried so deep in the waterfall.

You can now see that if we add up the amount of the loans, the equity investments, and your cash, all of the sources in your financing plan are here. The whole $500,000 is accounted for. Yet, with a market value of $500,000, there is a big problem! There are $70,000 in expenses at the top of the waterfall. All of your lenders are supposed to get back more than they put in. The money runs out even before your equity financier is fully repaid, and poor, dear, sweet Gramma gets nothing.

This! This is why your market value has to be bigger than your financing plan. Remember:

Market Value > Financing Plan > Budget

When your financing plan and your market value are equal, some of your investors are guaranteed to get burned. It is hard to imagine

Gramma (or any investor) being ok with this arrangement, knowing that the deck was stacked against her.

The next column over shows what happens if the market value of your film is $1 million. All of your lenders and financiers are repaid, all of your deferrals get paid out, and you recoup the cash that you spent. In addition, $74,500 flows to the profit participants. Everyone will be happy to get their check.

It turns out that all parties in priority positions 1 through 13 get fully repaid if the market value is at least $913,372 in this example. Please pause and think about that. In order to repay the investors and deferrals in this realistic scenario, the market value needs to be nearly double the financing plan in this example.

Furthermore, if the budget on the film is $450,000, then the market value of the film has to be more than two times the budget to repay all of the expenses and liabilities in priorities one through thirteen. If your market value and your budget are the same, then some of your financiers are guaranteed to lose money. The "greater than" symbol in the First Law of Film Finance is key to making your movies financially successful. Your investors will only have a reasonable chance of getting repaid if the market value is bigger than the financing plan, and the financing plan is bigger than the budget.

Your waterfall should not be in your business plan, because you will not know what it looks like yet. It is the result of completing your fundraising. You cannot know the investment amounts and the priorities within the waterfall until all of the contracts are negotiated and signed. Nonetheless, you should continually update a working draft of your waterfall for your reference as you go through the process of raising money for your film. As different pieces of the financing come on board, it will give you a map of where to go from here, and it will be useful in estimating your investor's return on investment.

Estimating Returns

> I'm focused on returning capital to investors.
> – Clay Pecorin, producer

Despite finance being a discipline that is focused on time – remember, we're time travelers! – there is no time shown in this waterfall. It could take five years from the start of production until your equity investor is repaid. In that time, they may have missed the opportunity to invest in the next *Knives Out*, because their money was still tied up in your film. Waterfalls like this are good at showing money, but not the time value of money. In other words, they downplay the actual risk for equity investors.

I want you to understand that your financing plan and your waterfall are linked. The financing plan is the before and the waterfall is the after. The financing plan is the projection of what you hope the waterfall will be. You can use the financing plan to project the rate of return that your investor will get if your film has the market value that you predicted.

Back in Chapter 3, we talked about investors expecting to earn a return. Just as they expect to earn a return on Netflix stock, they expect to earn a return on the money that they invest in your movie. Folks often talk about the ROI of a movie, which is short for return on investment. Your potential investors will almost certainly ask you about the ROI for your film too.

There are lots of different ways to calculate the return that an investor gets from your film. To keep things simple, I will focus on just two: the cash-on-cash return and the internal rate of return (IRR). Both of these are ways to measure ROI. The IRR is a superior method to cash-on-cash, but cash-on-cash is used far more often. I will explain why once I show you how each method works.

Cash-on-Cash

The goal of the cash-on-cash method is to show how much cash is expected to be returned in exchange for a $1 investment. Going back to the example of the lemonade stand from Chapter 3, your aunt invested $100, and then received $170 in return. We can calculate her cash-on-cash return as follows:

$$\text{Cash-on-cash} = \text{return} / \text{investment}$$
$$= \$170 / \$100$$
$$\text{Cash-on-cash} = 1.7$$

The answer of 1.7 tells us that your aunt received $1.70 for every dollar that she put into the lemonade stand. If your aunt's goal is to invest in more kids' lemonade stands, then the answer that we just calculated tells us that she can fund 1.7 more when she cashes out of yours. If she finds similar returns on those new investments, she can quickly grow a lemonade stand empire!

If the cash-on-cash return is exactly 1.0, then the investor gets back everything that they invested, to the penny. An answer greater than one means that the investor's cash is growing. We can see that in your aunt's cash-on-cash return of 1.7, with her cash growing from $100 to $170. If the cash-on-cash return is less than one, it means that the investor gets back less than they put in.

An investor in independent films is thinking about roughly the same thing. They usually want to invest in a bunch of movies, not just one. After all, the more they make, the more chances they have of being associated with an Oscar-winning film, meeting celebrities, and making a mark on society. Ideally, equity financiers also want their earlier investments to provide the cash for their later films. The goal is to invest in one movie, earn a return, and then put all of that money into another movie, earn another return, and then put all of that money into another movie, and so on. If it works right, the equity investor can make films for the rest of their life off that one first investment. Estimates of the cash-on-cash return from the waterfall tell them whether their pile of cash will grow or shrink.

We can calculate the cash-on-cash return for the equity investor in the waterfall earlier in this chapter. Luckily, we have two cases to work with, so we can see how the cash-on-cash return differs between them. In both cases, the equity financier invests $225,000 of cash. If the market value of the film is $500,000, then they get back $192,000 in priority #7, but nothing from their participations in priority #14. The cash-on-cash return is then:

Cash-on-cash = return / investment
 = $192,000 / $225,000
Cash-on-cash = 0.85

In this case, the investor gets back less than they put in. For every dollar they invest, they get back 85¢, which is money they could invest in another film. In very simple terms, the investor could invest in another 0.85 movies with the cash they get back. This is not the outcome the investor is hoping for.

Now we can recalculate the cash-on-cash return where the film's market value is $1,000,000 instead of $500,000. In that better case, the equity financier gets $270,000 back on their investment in priority #7, plus $27,938 from their participations in priority #14, for a total of $297,938. As a result:

Cash-on-cash = return / investment
 = $297,938 / $225,000
Cash-on-cash = 1.32

From the investor's perspective, a cash-on-cash return of 1.32 is better than 0.85, because it means they are getting back more money. To be thorough, when the film has that magical market value of $913,372, in which all of the investors get repaid as contracted but no participations are paid, then the cash-on-cash return to the equity financier is exactly 1.2. Thinking back to the 120 and 50, the cash-on-cash return of 1.2 is precisely the 120 piece of the equity investor's deal. Remember a cash-on-cash return of 1.2 says they will get back $1.20 for every dollar invested.

While the cash-on-cash method is widely used to project returns, it still ignores the time travel that financiers love. The cash-on-cash calculation lumps all of the money coming in and going out at the same point in time, and ignores how long it will take to get repaid. As a result, your equity investor cannot compare a projected cash-on-cash return on your film to the annual percentage return they are expecting from another investment opportunity. The alternative method to calculate returns that builds in the time lag is IRR.

IRR

IRR is the most widely used method in the corporate arena to estimate the return on new investments, but it is rarely used in film finance.[5] In summary, IRR solves for the percentage annual return over the entire life of the investment. This is really nice for investors, because it lets them compare an investment in your film to another investment on equal terms. If they know, for instance, the stock market might return 10% per year on average, then they can compare that to the return they will get from your movie.

Going back to the waterfall table, let's work with the numbers in the column in which your film has a market value of $1 million. You can see that your equity investor puts in $225,000, and then receives recoupment of $270,000 plus a participation payment of $27,938. Those do not happen at the same time. The investment happens at the start of production, the recoupment likely happens two years later, and the participation might be paid a year after that as the later windows begin to generate revenue.

The math behind IRR is really difficult and unnecessary to learn for your purposes, so we can use an online IRR calculator to do the heavy lifting for us. We can enter the numbers from the waterfall into an IRR calculator, and it will then tell us what annual return the investor would receive if all the amounts and timing work out as predicted. All IRR calculators use the exact same formula, so no one is better than the other. You can just do a search for "IRR calculator," and pull up hundreds of them that finance students use to cheat on their homework. Whichever you choose, you will enter the values as follows:

Initial investment (year 0) = 225,000
Year 1 = 0
Year 2 = 270,000
Year 3 = 27,938

Then hit the calculate button, and you should get an answer of 14.4%.[6] This means that your investor would be just as well off investing their

$225,000 for three years in another investment that guarantees a return of 14.4% per year. It also means that they will be much better off investing in your film than in a stock that pays 10% per year, assuming the film pays out as expected.

I strongly encourage you to pause here and try the IRR calculations for yourself so you can see how easy they are.

I will wait patiently. Maybe I will have a quick bite of something chocolatey. Really, please, take your time. Take your time.

OK.

You may be confused at this point, because your investor is guaranteed a 20% return in priority position #7, but the IRR comes out lower, at 14.4%. The key difference is that the IRR is an annual rate, so it is the average amount the investor would earn each year, including the participations. In contrast, the 20% premium is a lifetime rate, meaning that your equity financier would get a 20% return on their initial investment in total, ignoring the participations, and over the entire life of the film. These are not apples-to-apples comparisons.[7]

I love IRR because it is a simple answer to your investor's question of how much they will earn if the movie is a success. IRR is the best way to measure return on investment because it factors in the timing of when the cash is received. Unlike other ways that people estimate ROI, IRR is the only one that provides an annual return that lets the financier compare it to all other investment options before them, including stocks, mutual funds, and savings accounts.

The tricky part about IRR is that you are required to guess the timing of the cash flows. For instance, I guessed that the bulk of the cash generated by the film would arrive two years after the equity investor gave you their cash, and the rest would arrive a year after that. I picked numbers that could be realistic, but are not based on any contracts or discussions with sales agents/distributors for your film. The method of distribution will potentially change the timing of the cash flows. For instance, if your film gets acquired by a streaming service, and they pay in three equal payments over three years, then you would have different inputs to the IRR calculator. More traditional windows, moving from theatrical to free TV, will pay over many more years. As you are working with a sales agent to figure out the market value of your film, also talk through the most likely timing of the cash flows with them.

All of this information is presented to you in this section because you will hear potential investors talk about ROI, cash-on-cash returns, and maybe even IRR. It is important that you know what these are and how to have a conversation around them. My hope is that you will not look like a deer in headlights when these terms come up.

Sharing Estimated Returns

> Be honest about the risks.
>
> – Stu Pollard, producer

While it is important to know how to calculate hypothetical returns to equity so you can be fully engaged in the conversation, I strongly discourage you from ever sharing those estimates with potential investors. Just the act of providing possible financial outcomes is fodder for a lawsuit by your investors when your film does not perform as projected.

There are those that disagree with me. There is a very well-watched video on YouTube with an experienced producer explaining that he begins his pitch to investors with the ROI, and then tells them about the movie. Seemingly, this has worked for him, because he does not follow up with the story about the time he was wrong and the investors sued him. It makes sense too. If you can show an investor the potential upside of their investment, then it is much easier to make the case that they should feel like the risk they are about to undertake is reasonable.

In most industries, there is a decent chance that a new enterprise with a solid business plan will survive. Independent film is not like most industries. The financial outcome for most projects is a significant loss, and that fact is common knowledge. Legendary Hollywood attorney Schuyler Moore has written in Forbes that "Most films lose money. Indeed, 80% do."[8] Knowing that your film is very likely to not return your equity investor's cash, you put yourself in a precarious legal position when you begin your pitch or your business plan with a projection of the ROI. A wise investor will make their own estimates of returns anyway.

If you weigh the risks, and decide to present return projections to a potential investor, it may be best to calculate a separate IRR for several possible market values, and show them all to your investor, so you are not pinning yourself down to one number. For instance, maybe the film in my example has a market value of $500,000, instead of $1 million. In that case, the equity investor does not earn their full 20% premium, and the IRR is –7.6%. Or maybe there's a chance that the film will sell for $2 million, in which case the IRR would be 66.1%. As discussed in Chapter 10, the film could be worth $0, resulting in a complete loss for the investor, represented by the –100% in the table. A simple exhibit showing the range of possible outcomes, as shown in Table 11.2, will help reduce your legal risk. Also include the caveat that the returns are a projection based on assumptions about the budget, waterfall, distribution, and so many other elements of your film, and not guaranteed.

Table 11.2 Sample Returns Table

Market value	$0	$500,000	$1,000,000	$2,000,000
IRR	−100%	−7.6%	15.1%	66.1%
Cash-on-cash	$0.00	$0.85	$1.32	$2.76

In summary, your financing plan should include an estimate of the market value of the film, projections of your sources of cash (the pie chart), and a description of how you will mitigate the risk for the equity investors. I strongly discourage including an estimate of the equity investor's returns, but that is your call.

Takeaways

- Include a financing plan in your business plan to show potential partners how you expect to raise the funds for your film.
- Let potential investors know all of the ways that you intend to mitigate their risk.
- Always keep in mind the structure of the waterfall, and how much money will be left for you if the movie is a hit.

Notes

1 One of the producers I interviewed shot 13 films in Los Angeles, with budgets up to $20 million, all without guild involvement or interference.
2 The important variables affecting your residual payments to the guilds include which guilds you sign an agreement with, and which distribution sources generate revenue for your film (i.e. residual rates are higher on pay television than DVDs).
3 Historically, sales agents filled the role of collection account manager. However, many cases of impropriety showed the need for independent collection account managers, and Fintage House and Freeway were born. I strongly discourage the use of a sales agent as a collection account manager, because they inherently have a conflict of interest.
4 You may hear the terms "corridor" or "revenue corridor" used. A corridor gives a party the right to receive payment higher in the waterfall than would traditionally be expected. For instance, if you could get your deferred producer's fee moved up into the expenses part of the waterfall, instead of in the middle, that would be a corridor. These come about through negotiations with the financiers, and are rare.
5 A finance executive at a major studio once told me that they will not use IRR in their greenlight analysis because it would prove that they should not make most of the films on their slate, and then the studio would not need to exist and they would all lose their jobs.
6 I used https://www.calculatestuff.com/financial/irr-calculator to calculate the numbers for this example. The actual result from this calculator is

14.392%, and I rounded it to 14.4% for brevity. If you did not get 14.392% as the answer, then you probably need to enter −225,000 as the year 0 value. For clarity, that is a negative 225,000.

7 Ready for a little fun with math? You could calculate the IRR of the 20% premium only, using the same IRR calculator. Start by entering the $225,000 initial investment at Year 0, and the $270,000 cash flow in Year 2. Be sure to skip the participations payment in year 3. You will see that the 20% premium is not 20% per year. You should find an annual rate, or IRR, of 9.545%. This result means that an investor who earns 9.545% each year for two years will earn a 20% total return over two years. (Note that one might expect the annual rate to be 10%, because 10% + 10% = 20%. You can see the annual rate is less than 10%, and that happens because the investor is also earning interest on the interest from the first year.) If the $270,000 is not repaid until three years later, the IRR drops to 6.266%. The longer the investor has to wait to recoup their money, the lower the annual return that they earn.

8 "Most Films Lose Money!" Moore, Schuyler, Forbes.com, Jan. 3, 2019.

12 Equity in Independent Film

> Hollywood has always attracted money and always will.
> – Tim O'Hair, producer

Over the past century, rich people and their money have found their way to Hollywood. Joseph P. Kennedy, father of President John F. Kennedy, moved with his fortune from Boston to California in 1926 to take advantage of the invention of sound film. Just a year later, Howard Hughes took his sizable inheritance and his talents west to begin a career as a filmmaker. They've been coming ever since. The producers that I interviewed financed their films with the wealth of Silicon Valley billionaires, Wall Street tycoons, consumer products magnates, and industrial titans (and their heirs).

Wealthy individuals are just one of several sources of equity for your project. This chapter aims to show you all the different sources of equity, and the challenges of using equity to finance your film. The goal is for you to understand how it works in the real world, in today's world (or the today when I wrote this, which admittedly will be dated by the time I finish this sentence).

The job of equity in your financing plan is to meet the cash needs that debt and soft money can't meet on their own. While soft money does not need to be repaid, and debt usually has collateral attached, equity does not carry any guarantee of repayment. Furthermore, if a production runs out of money because of bad budgeting or planning choices, the hole can only be filled with equity. It is the riskiest form of investment.

To help give you some perspective, remember that independent films are widely known to be one of the worst investments in the world. Several producers acknowledged that they rank right near the bottom, along with Arabian horses and boats. Another producer quipped that the best way to get a million dollars out of an independent film is to start with $10 million. If you are going to raise money for your film, you are facing investors who are already biased toward believing that movies are awful financial investments.

Most equity investors fit neatly into one of the eight categories in Figure 12.1. The order of these eight categories is intentional. They go

128 Financing Your Film

Figure 12.1 Ranking Eight Categories of Equity Investors

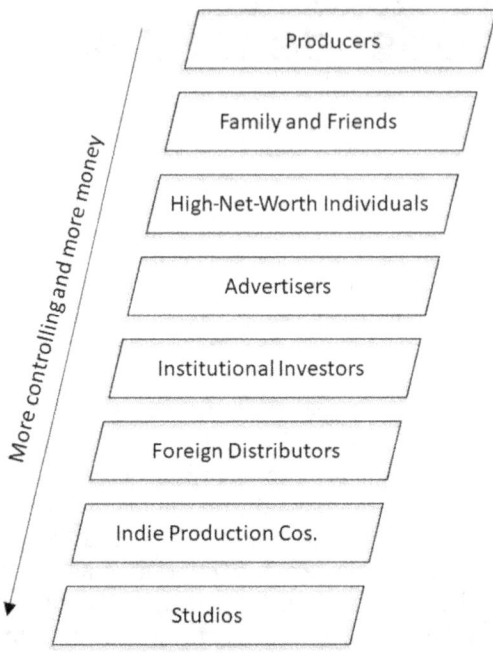

This figure shows eight categories of equity investors. They are ranked, with the categories at the top typically exerting less external control over the production, but also providing less money, than the categories at the bottom. Each category is defined in the text.

from #1, where the producers retain complete control over the film, to #8, where the producers may be completely shut out of the film. In general, when your friends and family give you money for your financing plan, they are not going to attach any strings. They will let you take the money and make your film as you see fit. John Baldecchi says, "If you're putting equity into the movie, you have a voice in the movie." That voice gets stronger as we move down through these eight categories.

High-net-worth individuals are number three on the list, because they may exert a little more control over the film. Often they will ask for a loved one to be cast in your movie. They will also ask to visit the set, but will typically not try to influence the production while there. Andrew Harvey, who built his career working as the production manager at Annapurna Pictures, will warn you, "The more you fill up the car, the more complicated it gets." If you get too many investors, you can end up with lots of small investors with control issues that can turn into a big problem.

Number four on the list, advertisers, joined the ranks of equity investors in recent years. Companies like Nike (through its Waffle Iron

Entertainment division) and Pepsi (Creator's League) realized that, instead of paying for a product placement and getting no backend, they could contribute a similar amount of cash through an equity investment, and get paid back if the film is a financial success. These advertisers are concerned with their product being glorified, and the story appealing to their target market. They also do not want to be associated with anything controversial. As a result, advertiser-investors are going to exert some control over the story and how the product is incorporated.

Institutional investors are fifth on the list. When these Wall St.-types come knocking with a suitcase full of cash, they might want even more control. However, institutions historically focused on major studio films, and are largely inactive in the independent film space now. You almost certainly will not gain an equity investment from a financial company today, including pension funds, insurance companies, hedge funds, private equity funds, and other Wall Street-type entities. However, every few years, a creative financial wizard invents a new way for institutional investors to get back into the movies, that promises to increase returns and decrease risk. We can expect something new any day now that could open new doors for you.

Foreign distributors are number six on the list, and make equity investments to help ensure that they have a pipeline of films to distribute. When they commit funds, they want to be sure that the movie will appeal to the audience in their territory. As a result, they may require certain cast, location, and story elements to seal the deal. One of my interview subjects shot a film in Thailand to make the distributor-investor happy, which thankfully ended up reducing the budget significantly.

The independent production companies, number seven on the list, usually come in one of two flavors. The first is an entity controlled by a wealthy individual that is run by experienced producers and makes investments in individual films. One such company is Participant Media, founded by the first employee and former president of eBay, Jeffrey Skoll, and run by former Universal Pictures chairman David Linde. They made several Oscar-winning films, including *An Inconvenient Truth*, *Green Book*, and *Judas and the Black Messiah*.

The second type of independent production company is the star-owned business, often with a first-look deal with a major studio. Examples include Jordan Peele's Monkeypaw, Brad Pitt's Plan B, and Reese Witherspoon's Hello Sunshine. Their first-look deals provide the studio with the right to see all of the independent production company's projects in development before they are shopped around to other buyers. In other words, these production companies already have their foot in the door, and access to lots of financing for the right projects.

The executives in both types of independent production companies almost certainly know more about the movie business than you, and will only invest in your film if they are allowed to make choices that they think will improve the odds of success for your film. In other words, they will demand a certain amount of control. However, there is such a huge spectrum of independent production companies, that there is a correspondingly huge gap in how much control any one of them might require.

Major studios are at the bottom of the list for a very good reason. If a major studio takes an equity position in your film, it may take complete control of it. The studio could install its own producers, reconfigure the talent, and make drastic changes to the script. It will insist on final cut. You might not have a role on the film going forward once a studio comes aboard.

If you want a lot of control, keep your equity investors to a select pool of family and friends. The downside is that you will probably need to work with a smaller budget. If you are comfortable giving control away to your equity financiers, then you can approach the categories of investors with lots more money lower down on this list.

These eight groups are all of the possible equity investors that I know of. These are the entities that you need to court to raise money over your career. They all have preferences about how they invest, based on factors like genre, their willingness (or not) to work with first time filmmakers, and how they structure their investments. As you get to know them, you will get to know their preferences and whether you are a good fit.

Amongst the producers I interviewed whose first film was not cash flowed or a negative pickup (see Chapter 3 if you forgot what those terms mean), 37% predominantly brought in the equity from themselves, family, or friends. Figure 12.2 shows that another 53% raised equity for their first film from high-net-worth individuals. The remaining 11% received a sizable equity investment from an independent production company, although all before 2004. Predictably, the average budgets on the first films bankrolled by wealthy individuals are higher than on those financed by the producers, their friends, or family. On the former, the average budget was $2.2 million, but only $364,000 on the latter.[1] These statistics point to the fact that you will almost certainly raise the equity for your first film from either your friends and family or high-net-worth individuals. Focus your energies on courting these two groups.

Later in your career, you may be able to leverage the agencies to help raise money. For instance, Marc Butan, producer of *Plane*, uses the help of talent agencies to gain introductions to new equity investors for all of his films now. To be clear, the talent agency does not raise money for the film or contribute their own money. Instead, their role is to play matchmaker between investors and producers. When the talent agency thinks a particular financier might be a good fit for a developing film, they will make an introduction. All of the negotiations

Figure 12.2 Comparing Sources of Equity

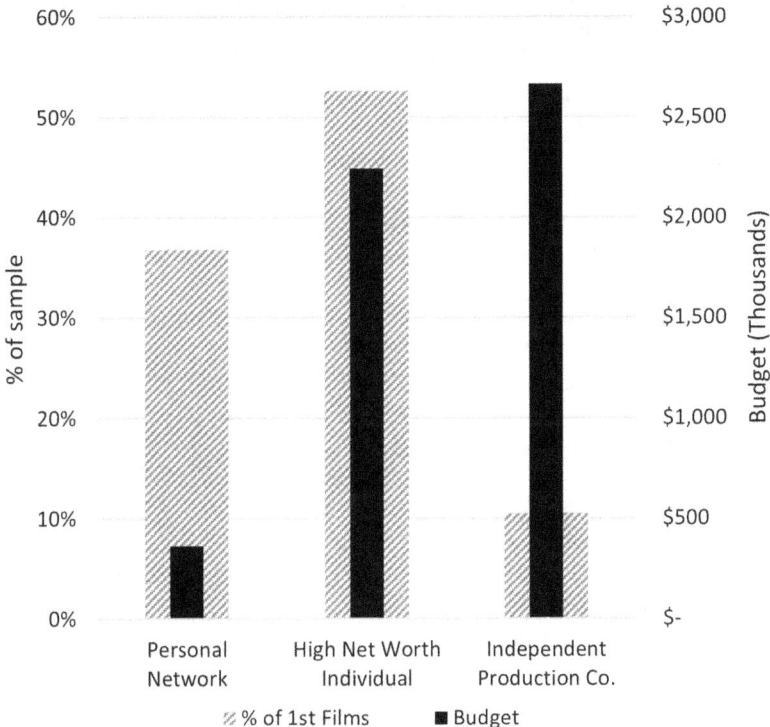

This chart shows a comparison of the primary sources of equity for producers' first films. It also shows a comparison of the average budgets for films primarily funded by each of the three sources. Personal Network includes funding from the producer themselves, their family, and their friends.

are held exclusively between the producers and the investors, with the agency out of the room.

Ross Putman leads the film finance team at the talent agency Verve. He described the agency's process as follows:

> It's pretty simple, but also pretty nebulous. The first step is that we want to make sure that the film can be as economically viable as possible. For me, that means having an understanding of what the market is like for finished films, having an understanding of what types of backend financials we're seeing for distribution deals, and applying that institutional knowledge, which hopefully I will have a lot more of than a random individual, because I'm at an agency and I've seen so many deals. Then we would go to the producers and say, "here's how much your movie should probably cost if you can do it for that. Here's how much an investor would probably feel comfortable risking, and here's how we can back up that information.

In other words, Mr. Putman is effectively walking producers through the First Law of Film Finance, given the current market conditions. "How much your movie should cost" is an estimate of the budget needed to make the film work under the Law. The financing plan is dictated by "how much an investor would probably feel comfortable risking." The final piece of the Law is market value, which Mr. Putman is able to estimate by "having seen so many deals."

Keep in mind, the goal of a talent agency is to secure acting roles for its clients. To get acting roles, they need to know which films have money. What better way to know than to help attach the money themselves.

All of the big talent agencies have film finance teams, and even some smaller ones do too. Mr. Butan told me that the agencies work with producers based on relationships. As they get to know you and your work, they are more likely to introduce you to financiers. His best advice for building a relationship with an agency: "don't ask them for something stupid." Mr. Butan also stressed that, "if you have a movie with a subject matter that is so fringe, so dark and depressing, or so obscure that nobody cares about it, then nobody can raise the money for you." The agencies understand what types of projects and producers are finance-able, and focus their energies on those targets.

In a bit of a plot twist, Mr. Putman first came into Verve as a client. On one of his films, another large agency had been introducing him to investors, but none of those meetings were turning into commitments. In the meantime, Verve signed the writer-director duo because they liked their work and wanted to represent them. As Mr. Putman tells the story, "we actually got a call out of the blue from an agent at Verve who said, 'I think I have money for you.' That was funny, because we hadn't asked them to find it. So it was really a great call to get, and certainly transformed my opinion of what was possible at an agency." Verve ended up as the sales agent on the film too, so this is a case of the introduction to the investor coming from one agency who represents both talent and sales.

I was surprised to learn in my interviews that sales agencies introduce equity investors to independent producers now too. Just as talent agencies are motivated by having a good pipeline of projects for their stars, sales agencies are motivated by having a good pipeline of films to sell to distributors. Producer Andrew van den Houten tells me that more and more, sales agencies take a separate fee when they make a match, even though they also get paid when they sell the movie. On other films, they will just take a larger share of the revenues when they bring in equity.

Getting financing through a sales agency or talent agency introduction is not something that comes easily. Amongst the producers that I interviewed, three-quarters tried to get an equity investment through a talent agency. Of those who tried, only about two thirds were successful. It is even less common to be matched to an equity investor by a sales agency, with only 17% of my interviewees finding cash that way. The rest had to find their equity investors elsewhere. Amongst those who were able to raise equity with the help of an agency, it happened on their fourth film, on average. You may still struggle to raise money through an agency even once your career takes off.

Four of the producers that I spoke with were able to raise equity with the help of a talent agency for their very first film. It was once possible, but probably is not anymore because of how much the movie business has changed over the past two decades. Those four films had an average budget of about $10 million, but most were released before 2002.

Why Equity?

> Every equity investor has their own reason for doing it.
> – Scott Einbinder, producer

Is equity necessary? We can get further into the data so that you can see how producers finance their films over the course of their careers.

Let's begin at the beginning, with the first feature that each producer got financed. Among those first films, 73% were entirely financed by equity. In other words, these producers could not use debt, tax incentives, grants, product placements, or any other means to complete their budget. All that they had at their disposal was equity. 73%! Raising equity is a wall that almost all producers must climb to establish their career.

The benefit of data is that it lets us see the big picture, without all the crazy anecdotes. In this case, we can see that you are almost certainly going to need to raise a lot of money through equity to get your first movie made. Even the films that were not entirely financed by equity used thousands of dollars of equity, and in some cases millions, to meet their budget. If you want to produce your first movie, you need to steel yourself for the hustle of finding equity investors.

The 27% of first films that were not entirely equity financed largely used presales and negative pick-ups to complete their budgets. For instance, when John Baldecchi went about the process of building the pile of cash he needed to make *The Mexican*, he lined up presales to cover about one-sixth of the budget. Again, separating anecdotes from data, this is not a typical example of a first film. Brad Pitt and Julia Roberts starred in it. The budget was allegedly $57 million. Mr. Baldecchi spent many years working under the wing of *Jerry Maguire* producer Laurence Mark before striking out on his own, so he was already known and trusted in the community. While it is possible to use presales to partially finance your first film, the data suggests that it is unlikely.

Raising a lot of equity seems to be a rite of passage for new producers. After all, the institutional parts of the independent film financial system will only trust that you can complete a feature once you show them that you have completed a feature. For instance, sales agents and distributors see way too many producers at their door to take a risk on each one. Filtering out the first-time producers is an easy way to narrow down the pool.

If the institutional financial parties will not place a bet on you, and your friends and family cannot contribute enough, then you may need to turn to parties who measure investing success in different terms – high-net-worth individuals. Whereas lenders only measure success by how much money they made off your film, wealthy individuals might use different measures of success. Producers interviewed for this study identified four alternative motives for high-net-worth individuals to contribute capital to films:

Social change: The message of the film is closely aligned with the morals of the investor, and they are hoping that a large audience will receive that message and change their behavior. An example of an investor focused on social change is Participant Media, mentioned earlier.

Quite a few of the producers that I spoke with raised money for a single film by working with a group of investors who had an affinity for a topic. Bill Borden financed the Spike Lee film *Get on the Bus* through a group of African-American businessmen, who wanted to see the story of the Million Man March told in a movie. Bill MacDonald raised the money for Snoop Dog's *Grow House* from a half-dozen investors that he described as "an interesting, eclectic group who are supporting marijuana as a recreational matter."

Social life: Even before committing capital to a movie, a potential investor is invited to meals and parties with actors, directors, writers, and producers. (One producer interviewed for this study flew the Oscar-nominated lead actress to sing for a group of potential investors at a party in Texas.) Once invested in the film, the financier often gets to visit the set during filming and attend the red carpet premiere. If the film does well, they could also get to attend film festivals and awards shows. Many equity partners see the cost of investing as the price of admission to the Hollywood lifestyle.

Leaving a legacy: Ever since the Medici family in Renaissance Italy crafted their legacy through their support of artists including Leonardo da Vinci and Michelangelo, other wealthy families have tried to do the same. Some wealthy investors view investments in film as a way to leave their legacy, moreso than as a means to grow wealth. To solidify that legacy, they will ask for credits on the films they select for investment. It will be up to you to negotiate whether your equity financiers are credited as producer, executive producer, or something else. You will also need to agree on the methods by which credits are publicized (on the movie poster, in the trailer, in the opening or closing credits, and so on).

Acting roles: While few investors hope to be in front of the camera someday, their children, spouses, and significant others often aspire to make it big in Hollywood. Many producers are met with the offer of an equity investment in exchange for putting a financier's loved-one in front of the camera. To be clear, there is a potential future financial payoff to the actor (or those financially supporting them) from getting a paid acting role on a union-supported movie. Many casting directors are looking for actors with work experience, so landing that first acting job may open the door to other acting jobs. Also, once a performer has worked a paid speaking role on a film covered by the actors' union, SAG-AFTRA, they are able to join the union and potentially also receive healthcare benefits.[2]

* * *

You can improve your odds of successfully raising equity by learning your investor's motivations, and then playing to them. Milan Chakraborty suggests that you, "don't take a one size fits all approach to your pitches." Your business plan should highlight the social change, social life, legacy, and acting role opportunities for investors, as appropriate. Similarly, you can figure out if a potential investor is a bad fit through learning their values as well. If they are insistent on their son getting a meaty role in your film focused on four girls stuck in a cave, then you know that you need to move on and find other sources of equity (although that investor might be a good fit for another film in your pipeline). However, in the words of *Plus One* producer James Short, "Don't just tell investors what you think they want to hear. That's a trap." You may find your movie stuck with an investor who has strongly different opinions than you, and compromising in ways that really hurt the final product.

High-net-worth individuals are not sitting on their McMansion front porches, with buckets of cash, waiting to give them away to any 21-year-old with a film degree. But they are more willing to take risks on first-time producers than banks and major studios because of their different definitions of investment success. The world will not run out of these potential financiers anytime soon. *A Day to Die* producer Andrew van den Houten insists that "there will always be an investment base if you're good enough to sell the idea."

Normally, the big risks for equity investors in independent films are whether the producer will complete the film and if they can find competent distribution. Equity investors can reduce their risks by investing in experienced producers, who have a track record of actually completing films and monetizing them through distribution. When a wealthy investor makes an investment in a producer's first film, they are taking a risk on both. Given that the novice producer has no track record of completing films and securing competent distribution, the investor is taking a giant leap of faith.

You can be creative about how to sweeten the pot for potential equity investors to incentivize them. Your equity investor will almost certainly ask for ownership of a share of the IP, so they will be compensated further if there is a sequel or spin-off. Producer Ricky Fosheim is a big believer in giving your very first equity investors a piece of your second movie too, even if it is from completely different IP. In his mind, if you're going to benefit from all of the learning that happens with a first film, then your investors should too. Contractually, this can be tricky, because you probably do not know what your next movie will be yet, or how much of it you will have available to give away. If your investor is willing to trust you with their money, then hopefully they are also willing to trust your handshake agreement for the next film too.

Milan Chakraborty advises producers to "always play the long game." By that, he means that you should treat every potential financier as though they will eventually invest in one of your films. Stu Pollard similarly told me that, "we meet people, we like them, and making something together is a long-term goal." All investors need the time to make sure they are committing their hard-earned cash to the right project, in some cases over ten years after first meeting the producer. High-net-worth individuals especially need time, and they often also need their family business to be healthy enough to allow them to dabble on the side in film. As you get to know a potential financier, you also get to know their investment process, which eventually gives you an inside track to securing their commitment.

As much as I tried to get a good understanding of how producers meet high-net-worth individuals through my interviews, I got an awful lot of vague responses like "I just met her around" or "maybe from someone I know." Generally, what these responses mean is that the producers are really good at talking to anyone and everyone, all the time. I will talk more about this in later chapters. Just one quick piece of advice from Arclight Film's Chief Financial Officer, Brian Beckmann: "once you find them, you need to take care of them."

* * *

I asked lots of questions to the narrative feature producers that I interviewed for this book about their first films, because I really wanted to understand how they started their careers. Those first films are unique for so many reasons. The budgets on the first films they produced on their own are smaller than you might expect. The median first film budget is just $1 million. (Median means that I sorted the list of 50 first film budgets from largest to smallest, and $1 million is exactly halfway down the list. The bottom of the list is a $4,000 movie, and the top is a number I am not allowed to share.)[3] In comparison, when asked about the budget on their second film, the median response was $1.4 million.

First films are also different in that the funds used to pay for developing the script and getting the project off the ground (i.e. the development funds) are almost always from the producer, the director, the writer, or their parents. On their most recent films, development funds came from studios, streamers, production companies, and equity investors.

Eighty-six percent of the budget is funded by equity on the average first film. In comparison, producers use equity for 70% of the budget of their second films. It is exciting to know that second films use less equity as a percentage of the budget, even though their budgets are bigger. As shown in Figure 12.3, producers are raising more money,

Figure 12.3 Comparing 1st and 2nd Films

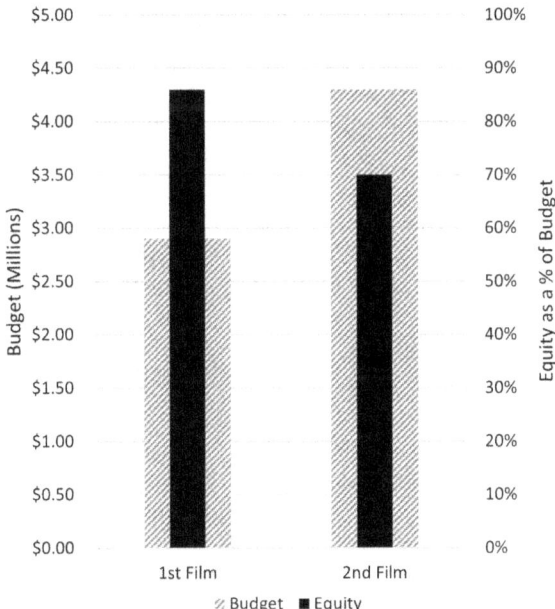

This chart shows a comparison of the budgets of producers' first films and second films. It also shows a comparison of the percentage of the budget that was funded by equity between the two films.

and more of that money is coming from non-equity sources. The second films' budgets are larger because more than half used tax incentives. Producers typically begin to use debt on their third film, as they borrow against presales and tax incentives. We will dig into these statistics even more in Chapter 13.

All of these statistics suggest that raising money gets easier after the first film. If you are like the typical first-time producer, then the first film that you make on your own will be small and really hard to finance. If you build it following the First Law of Film Finance and your investors recoup, then you will begin to build your financial track record. In the words of *Flower* producer Eric Fleischman, "My ability to raise capital is contingent on my financial track record. It changes the way the industry views you." Many of my interviewees told me that first-time producers whose films make money then go on to make bigger budget projects. Those who lose money do not.

Leaps of Faith

> Now you're more required to take a leap of faith.
> – Rob Barnum, producer

I want to come back to two key thoughts from earlier. The first is the idea that investors let their money time travel with you, by giving you some cash today that will be repaid with interest in the future, from the revenue generated by your film. The second is that nobody actually knows the amount of revenue that your film will earn before it is released.

When we combine these two concepts, we're left with the conclusion that investors are giving you money today in hopes that enough revenue is generated to repay them, but they do not know if that will be the case when they invest. Your investor has to take a leap of faith, and hope it works out.

Finance is an entire discipline built on leaps of faith. For instance, when you buy a house someday, you will do the math to figure out how much your monthly payment and other expenses will be, you will make guesses about how much money you will earn in the future, and then you will take a leap of faith and sign the papers. You might get fired the next week and lose your house, or you might get a producing deal with HBO Max that lets you afford a much nicer house in a better neighborhood. Either way, you don't know the future, so you have to take a leap of faith.

Similarly, the bank is taking a leap of faith when they give you the loan. They know very little about what your future holds, but enough to take the risk. Your lender could very easily lose thousands and thousands of dollars on your home loan. Yet, if they did not make your loan and many others just like it, they would not have a reason to exist. The bankers would lose their jobs (and maybe their homes too). Their business is built on making careful, calculated leaps of faith.

In fact, the finance team at every corporation is tasked with helping the CEO make leaps of faith. When Disney bought Fox for $71 billion, Disney made a bet that it would get that $71 billion back plus interest. So far, that leap of faith worked out. The same could be said about Google's legendary purchase of YouTube for $1.65 billion, which generated $29 billion of ad sales in 2021 alone. In contrast, the American phone company Verizon's purchase of internet dinosaur Yahoo for $4.5 billion is a leap of faith that did not work out. They sold the scraps of Yahoo four years later for very little money.

Your investor knows that they are taking a leap of faith with you when they commit. They know that they might hit the ground hard. It is your job to make them comfortable with the uncertainty of the future. We will talk more about that in the chapters to come.

The Moral Burden of Equity

> I don't like the feeling of not getting investors repaid.
> – Clark Peterson, producer

Despite the fact that nearly all producers rely on equity to build their careers, a sizable pool of producers also struggle with the moral burden of equity. Once you accept money from a financier, you will feel the weight of it on your shoulders every day until you repay it. In some cases, you will never get them their money back.

I can offer some data to assess how risky independent films are for equity investors. I asked my interview subjects what percent of their films recouped for their equity investors, which is a fancy way to say that the investor got back all of the money that they put in. In other words, if an investor contributed $25,000 to the budget, and then got back $25,000 when the film sold to HBO, then that investor recouped.

Amongst successful producers who were willing to answer the question, 39% of their films recouped for the equity investors on average. Your first instinct when reading that sentence may be optimistic (there's a 39% chance my investors will get all of their money back!) or pessimistic (the glass is less than half full). Savvy investors who know finance will read that number and be terribly disappointed, and let me explain why.

First, a quick look at one source of bias through sports. Imagine a stadium packed almost entirely with home team fans. If an alien landed on Earth and only saw the stadium, then they would assume that the vast majority of people support the home team. Their perspective would be biased because they never saw the visiting team's stadium when it was full too.

Just as the stadium attendance is biased towards the observable fans, so is my estimate of the percent of films that recouped for their equity investors. Notice that the 39% figure is only sourced from producers who were willing to answer the question. (There was a noticeable amount of squirming many times when I asked this question, so I usually asked it towards the end of the interviews.) Presumably, producers who are proud of their record of recouping for their equity investors would be more willing to answer (the home team fans), and those who were disappointed in their record would be less willing (the visiting team's fans). Therefore, I do not have responses from everyone in this statistic. Furthermore, the folks who are disappointed probably recouped on less than 39% of their films. Therefore, I am missing the producers who recouped on less than 39% of their films from my statistic. The real value is likely less than 39%.

Second, the people answering the question are successful producers, who all completed at least four films. Including younger producers with fewer films under their belts and other producers who never got a second chance would also make it less than 39%.

Third, remember that equity investors want to earn interest on their money over time. If they simply wanted to get their money back three years later, they could just put it in the bank. They are taking the risk on independent film because they want to earn interest on their money. The estimate that 39% of films recoup for their equity investors also says that equity investors –at best – earned interest on 39% of films. The vast majority of equity investors would be better off leaving their money in the bank.

All told, the percentage of independent films that recoup for their equity investors is likely much lower than 39%. My guess is that the only people who know the correct percentage with any degree of precision are the collection account managers Freeway and Fintage. They receive all of the revenues from an independent film, and then distribute the money through the waterfall under the terms that each debt and equity investor agreed to with the producers.[4] The collection account managers do this work for hundreds of independent films each year, and get to see how much equity investors and profit participants get paid. Unless Freeway and Fintage find a way to release their data, we will never know the exact number, but it is certainly lower than you or I would like.[5]

Successful producers often become scarred over time by not being able to get their equity investors' money back on a particular film. Many devised means to help them cope with the moral burden of equity. Lisa France, producer of the tear-jerking documentary *Roll with Me*, demands that her equity investors "prove it won't hurt you or your family." She actually asks potential investors to show documentation to indicate that they have enough money to bear the loss comfortably.

Similarly, other producers find peace with the moral burden of equity by requiring a particularly high-net-worth amongst the high-net-worth individuals that they are courting. Dimitri Logothetis told me that he only accepts "money from people worth $100 million, not people worth $2 million." By setting such a high bar, he is confident that any losses will not significantly hurt the investing family.

Still other producers are turning to television as a means to get away from equity funding. Almost all television shows are funded by the network or streaming platform. That production will almost always be cash-flowed or take the shape of a negative pick-up, where the producers get a loan based on the contract with the network. (I am told that Netflix used to do that a lot, until all the entertainment banks in Los Angeles decided that they had too many loans backed by Netflix in their portfolios.) Either way, there is no need to raise equity from outsiders, and thereby, no risk in losing an equity investor's cash.

The good news for you is that most equity investors have some sense of just how risky the movie business is before they commit. High-net-worth individuals are willing to take the risk because they get more out of it than just a financial ROI. There are many producers that I interviewed who built their careers off of equity, and continue to use lots of equity to get their films made. As *Couples Night* producer Chuck West told me, "equity is a great opportunity to build."

Equity can have a criminal side that all producers need to manage carefully. There is a history of crooks who invested their ill-gotten gains in movies. This goes far beyond small independent films. Even *The Wolf of Wall Street*, starring Leonardo DiCaprio and directed by Martin Scorsese, was allegedly financed with money being laundered from a Malaysian development fund.[6] Several of my interview subjects inadvertently worked with financiers who later went to jail. One in particular mentioned that "there are so many crooks out there, that ruin it for decent producers that care about their investors." Producer James Short will tell you, "be careful who you take money from." If your film is stained by investment with stolen money, it may not be able to get distribution. Similarly, you may not be able to find partners who want to work with you again.

* * *

But wait, there's more! The moral complications of equity do not stop there. As producer Milan Chakraborty explained to me, "the worst thing that you can do for the ecosystem is raise money before you're ready for it." That is a nice way of saying that if you lose money for your investor, they will never invest in your films again, and probably will not invest in anyone else's projects either. Investors will typically try again only if they made money the first time. If you do not get them repaid their first time, they probably will not come back. There is a sense that you have a responsibility to both the equity investor and all other independent filmmakers. If your investor does not get repaid, you inflict damage upon both groups.

Equity in the Age of Streaming

> The risk profile relative to the upside can be very frustrating.
> – Rob Barnum, producer

Equity investors face a very different set of risks today, as streaming video services like Amazon Prime, Hulu, and Netflix are releasing so many films. It seems at first blush like new buyers in the marketplace would be beneficial, but that is not always the case for the equity investors.

When a movie is released theatrically, the equity investors are positioned to earn seemingly endless amounts of money if it is a hit. For instance, a little-known British equity fund called Ingenious Media seems to have invested £46 million in an equity position in James Cameron's *Avatar*. Due to the enormous box office success, Ingenious is reported to have collected £250 million in profits (the bottom line of the income statement).[7] Big payoffs like that encourage equity investors to take the risk.

These days, if a film goes straight to a streaming platform without a theatrical release, then there is no unpredictable upside, and no chance for a big payoff. Streaming services typically pay for the production cost plus a mutually agreed profit margin. The profit margin is independent of how successful the film is on the streaming platform. More views do not result in more profit for the producer and the investors. For the equity investor in a film with a streaming distribution deal, the interest they earn on their investment is guaranteed but small.

Remember, finance is about risk and return. For equity investors who are intentionally taking on a lot of risk, a guaranteed small return of interest is actually hurtful, because it blocks the potential to receive *Avatar*-sized returns. Investors who are putting up money without distribution already in place are taking bigger risks than before, but with much lower payoffs because the theatrical market has shrunk so much. That is what Rob Barnum means when he says, "The risk profile relative to the upside can be very frustrating."

The shift in the distribution marketplace has definitely amped up the risk for equity investors. The rise of streaming brought about the fall of theatrical releases for independent films. In addition, the special projects of the on-screen stars used to be produced independently. Now, the talent can go to a streamer and get their prestige projects made, so the indie producers do not have access to big stars like they used to. The combination of the withering of independent theatrical releases and the shortage of talent means the presales market has shriveled to a fraction of its former size. Producers now only have a handful of buyers who might agree to distribute their film while it is still in development. Jeff Sackman admitted that, in the current marketplace, "the best deal is to sell to Netflix or Amazon or a streamer like that." Similarly, Bill Borden told me, in only slightly exaggerated terms, "there are only four buyers left in the market. If all four pass, you're done." In that case, the producer has to make a tough choice. They can either abandon the project altogether, or try to make it without distribution in place, and hope that it will sell once completed.

These changes in the distribution landscape have also given rise to more backstop deals. A backstop deal is essentially a presale, which gives the producer the option to find a higher bidder after the film is complete. If that white knight appears and is willing to buy your finished film for a higher price, then you will need to pay a kill fee to the original distributor that provided the backstop. If not, then the film will get distribution through the backstopper. The amount of the kill fee is part of your negotiation, and not set in stone. While backstop deals are helpful in greenlighting your project, the kill fees can reduce the payouts to equity investors, because the money is going to the backstopping distributor instead of your waterfall.

The evolution of streaming has increased the risk and lowered the returns to equity, thereby making it harder to attract investors. You will hear experienced producers bemoan this shift in the business, on panels, on Twitter, in happy hours, and anywhere else they have a platform to speak. Their disappointment is understandable, because the easier way of doing business that they used to have available to them has mostly disappeared. When you hear those complaints, you have an important choice to make. You can throw everything in the trash, and walk away from your independent film entirely. Or you can pause to recognize that independent movies are still getting financed every single day. Despite the increased financial risks, people still want to be making movies for other reasons. Raising equity has never been easy, but it is still possible, and within your reach.

How You Treat Your Investors Matters

Treat money well so they come back later.

– Tim O'Hair, producer

> Be as responsible as possible so that hopefully we can form more long-lasting partnerships.
>
> – Ross Putman, producer and agent

I could go on. So many of the producers that I interviewed for this book had something to say about treating their investors well. Importantly, this is not just your job. Naomi Despres, producer of *Kill the Messenger*, advises that, "your producing partners need to share the same sense of responsibility to the financiers." You all have a duty and a career interest in treating your investors well.

Some of the wisest advice about how to treat your investors came from one of the youngest producers that I interviewed. Jason Tamasco has been very successful getting the same investors to take bets on several of his films. He stresses that you need to "make sure your investors enjoy working with you." That means you need to treat them professionally, keep them updated as often as possible, and get their input on important decisions. Mr. Tamasco also stresses the importance of "sharing bad news fast." It does not do you or your investors any good to hold back bad news or sugar coat it. Let them know the bad news when you find out, and let them have the same time as you to process it and make informed decisions going forward. They will respect you much more if you don't hide the bad news.

Many of the producers that I spoke with stressed that equity investors are smart people who understand the risk they are taking when they put money into your film, and they have already spent a lot of time considering the possibility that they will not get repaid. Bad news is the most likely outcome and is expected, so you do not need to shy away from it. I will very intentionally not name names for this anecdote, but quite a few of my interview subjects lost money for an investor, only to have that same person put equity into the producer's next film. The investors came back because they saw the professionalism of the producer, and had faith that they would make their best effort to complete a financially-viable film. Sharing bad news is not necessarily the end of your relationship with your investor.

Takeaways

- You will almost certainly need to raise equity for your first film, and lots of it, knowing that there is a reasonable chance that those investors will not get their money back.
- There are lots of different types of equity investors. Get to know the motivations of your potential investors to make sure you are a good match.
- Treat your equity investors well so that they will want to work with you again.

Notes

1 As a tease for what is coming in the next chapter, producers whose equity came from wealthy individuals worked about 10 years before producing their first film, whereas the "family and friends" producers only worked about two years before making their first movie.
2 See: https://www.sagaftra.org/membership-benefits/steps-join
3 The average first film budget, $2.85 million, is misleading in this case because it is skewed upward by that huge number I cannot share. Only 22% of the first films had a budget of $2.85 million or more. The median tells us that half had a budget of $1 million or more.
4 The contract that specifies how the film's revenues are to be distributed is called the Collection Account Management Agreement, or CAMA (pronounced just like the word 'comma'). You will hear people talk about the CAMA a lot, because it is so important for investors and producers who want to be paid.
5 I asked Fintage's co-CEO, Robbert Aarts, if it was possible to release the data. He gave me a long, reasonable list of all of the reasons why they couldn't. I'm happy to know they at least considered it.
6 See: https://www.hollywoodreporter.com/news/general-news/1mdb-scandal-documents-reveal-link-scorsese-s-wolf-wall-street-1244217/
7 https://deadline.com/2010/05/profile-of-avatar-co-financer-ingenious-the-fallout-after-uks-tax-man-cometh-39314/

Part 3
Beyond the Basics

Do you remember that scene in *The Matrix*, when Trinity and Neo are standing on top of a building under dark clouds, as a helicopter looms large in the background? Neo asks, "Can you fly that thing?" Trinity calls in to the operator on an old Nokia cell phone to retrieve a pilot program for a B-212 helicopter. Tank uploads the information into her brain, and then, a few eye flutters later, Trinity can fly it.

There are so many moments when I wished that technology existed. There are so many times that I just want to upload the new information into my brain, and then get to work. However, even if there was something like that for film finance – even if you could instantly sync all of the information in this book right into your brain – you still would not be ready to finance your first film.

My interviewees made it perfectly clear to me that there is so much more to completing film financing than just the academic basics. In the brief chapters that follow, I share some of their wisdom about all of the other things that matter when trying to finance a movie.

13 Experience Matters

> People will only trust you to make your movie if you have proven that you can handle the job. Equity investors will only hand over their wealth if they believe in the project and believe in you.
>
> – Jason Tamasco, producer

This might be the most useful chapter in this whole book. To set the table, this is a chapter about work experience, in a book about finance. As you will see, there is a deep connection between experience and finance amongst independent film producers. There is no single key to unlock the financing for your movie, but this chapter provides the closest thing that I can offer you to that illusory key.

When I started on this book, I naively thought that most successful independent producers graduated from film school, and then just started making their own movies.

Boy, was I wrong.

The most surprising thing that I learned by interviewing producers is that only six out of 50 had gone straight from film school to making movies, without working for someone else first. The average lifetime worldwide box office generated by those producers' films is about $8 million, far less than the $36 million average for all fifty producers.

There is tremendous value to learning how business works, inside a company, from a boss, before striking out on your own. John Baldecchi, producer of *The Mexican*, would say that on-the-job experience teaches you "how to get your voice heard but not get shot in the back of the head." My producer-subjects gained their capabilities in so many different ways. By far the most common work experience: about one-third of the producers worked in an office, supporting the production of films, before making their own movie. They did not just do a short stint, learn the ropes, and then leave. The median time spent working before they made their first movie was eight years. Think about that – successful producers spent eight years learning under someone else's wing before flying out on their own.

DOI: 10.4324/9781003363446-17

That was only one-third of my producers. Another third had a wide set of different experiences within the entertainment industry. Six worked on set or in post-production. Three worked for sales or distribution companies. Two worked in studio finance and another two were working writers.

The remaining third of my sample did not have significant experience in entertainment before becoming a producer. Five came from Wall Street, where they were investment bankers, savaging the world of high finance. Zaheer Goodman-Bhyat learned to trade foreign currencies in that role, which later allowed him to save one of his films from financial crisis.[1] Another two were practicing attorneys.

There is also a fascinating batch of entrepreneurs in my group. Scott Einbinder started a brick-and-mortar surf shop in Orange County, California while still in college. He knew his customers, built a successful business, and grew. Before long, he was looking to raise millions of dollars from savvy financiers to open a lot more stores. Suddenly he was hiring investment bankers, making financial projections, weighing his options of taking investment through debt versus equity, and being grilled by potential investors. It may have been the perfect training ground for independent producing. Surprisingly, Mr. Einbinder was producing films the whole time, while also running the surf shop enterprise.

Other entrepreneurs cashed out of another business before becoming a producer. Bill MacDonald sold off his jelly sandal company and went to Mexico to retire as a young man. Luckily, his neighbor was the Oscar-winner John Huston, who convinced him to get into the movie business. Robert Barnum merged his tech company with another, took his gains and his business acumen, and became a successful producer. Brad Zions was lucky enough to be an early employee at America Online. The entrepreneurial mindset is critical to success in producing independent films, although you can clearly make a lot more money in other industries.

I am also a huge fan of the work experience that Maurice Fadida gained while he was young. Mr. Fadida managed residential construction projects. Like a producer, he had to keep his crew happy while managing sometimes irrational homeowners (the talent). He had to deal with budgets, deadlines, permits, accounting, and pipelines of work. Mr. Fadida learned that putting out fires is not the best way to run a business. As he told me, "good producers are problem solvers, but the best producers are problem preventers."

Of all of the work experiences of the producers that I interviewed, I am most endeared by that of Jason Tamasco. Straight out of college, he worked for a staffing agency, and his job was to cold-call nurses to try to get them to take an open position. In that role, he had to listen to nurses complain endlessly about their last 16 jobs, and try to be reassured that this one would be better. Mr. Tamasco also learned to sell himself over the phone to people who did not know him. It turns out that listening to concerns and selling your ideas to other people are skills that come in really handy when meeting with investors.

The optimistic takeaway from all of these different experiences is that there is no one best career path to becoming an independent film producer. The most important thing is that you develop a good skill stack somewhere along your journey that will benefit you and complement your producing partners' talents. *Bread and Butter* producer Stephen Gibler told me, "you have to have specific talent that separates you from the rest of the pack." *The Butterfly Effect* producer A.J. Dix echoed that sentiment when he told me that new filmmakers need to "bring something to the party."

Albert Nobbs producer Julie Lynn emphasizes the importance of working hard to get noticed in your early jobs. Her advice: "Whatever you're asked to do, do it to the best of your ability."

Taking the time to develop your skill stack, build a network of connections, and grow credibility is critical to your career success. Thanks to data, I can tell you just how important experience is for your career. I split my producers into two nearly-equal groups – those who worked more than eight years before producing their first film independently, and those who worked less than eight years. For convenience, I will call those with more than eight years of work experience "more-trained," and those with less than eight years the "less-trained." There are 26 producers in the more-trained group, and 24 are less-trained.

The more-trained producers appear to have more successful careers on so many levels. To help show that, I use medians in the paragraphs that follow instead of averages. To find a median, all of the numbers are sorted from smallest to biggest, and then the median is the number right in the middle of the list. Medians are more reliable than averages in cases when there is one huge number on the end of the list that makes the average much bigger than it would be otherwise. That huge number is called an outlier. Amongst my producers, there are outliers in budgets and box office sales. If I showed you averages instead of medians, my conclusions would still be the same.

The more trained producers get to work with bigger budgets faster. On the first films that they produced independently, the median budget for the more-trained group is about $2.3 million, but only $500,000 for the less-trained. On the second film that they made independently, the less trained get a median budget of $900,000, while the more-trained spend $4.5 million. Even on their current features, the more-trained are working with median budgets of $11 million, versus $2.4 million for the less-trained. The more-trained start with bigger budgets, and continue with bigger budgets.

The more-trained producers may get more money to work with because of where they find it. Amongst my producers, only one-quarter financed their first film with money from themselves, friends, and family. In contrast, half of the less-trained producers had to use those close contacts to fund their first films. Similarly the more-trained were about seven times more likely to presell their first and second film than the less-trained. By being able to tap into high-net-worth and institutional sources of equity, as well as presales, earlier in their careers, the more-trained were able to achieve bigger budgets faster.

The more-trained producers also have bigger lifetime box offices. The median is $12 million for the more-trained group, and $580,000 for the less-trained.[2] It should be noted that those differences are not driven by when they released their first films. Both groups released their first film in 2005, on average.

More experience also translates to more impactful films. I measure how socially impactful each film is by counting how many votes it received on the popular movie data website, IMDB.com. I cannot just compare the votes of the more-trained to the votes of the less-trained, and call it a fair fight. The less-trained have more years to make movies, because they jump in at a younger age. As a result, the less-trained make more movies (about three more on average, at the

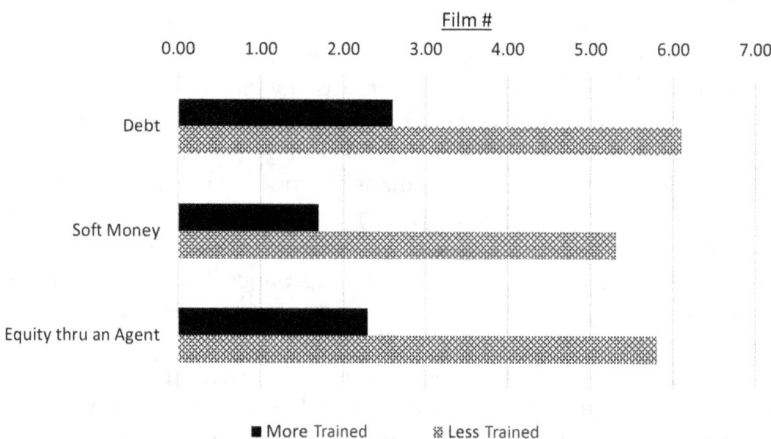

Figure 13.1 How Fast Do Producers Reach Sophisticated Financing Sources?

This figure shows how quickly the average producer in the sample of 50 uses various, sophisticated financing sources in their career. The Film # represents which movie in the sequence of their career was the first to use a specified source. Debt includes all types of loans. Soft money includes tax incentives, grants, and other sources described in the text. Equity thru an Agent indicates that an equity financier was introduced to the producer by a sales agent or talent agent. More trained producers worked at least eight years before making their first feature. Less trained producers worked less than eight years.

time I interviewed them). There is some fancy math involved here, but I will spare you the details and get to the punchline.[3] All else equal, more-trained producers received about 93,000 more votes on their library of films than less-trained producers.

All of these differences seem to be driven by finance. If we peek at how quickly the two groups of producers moved away from those 100% equity-financed first films made on spec, we can see that the experienced producers moved along faster. For instance, Figure 13.1 shows that the more-trained group were using debt on their third film, on average, whereas the less-trained producers waited until their sixth. Given that presales are driven by talent, it may be taking the less-trained group more time to land stars for their films.

Similarly, the less-experienced group waited until their fifth film to use soft money, whereas the more-experienced got there three films faster. Soft money often becomes accessible once budgets reach a critical size and productions move out of Los Angeles. I showed earlier that the more-experienced producers get bigger budgets faster.

When it comes to raising equity with the help of a talent or sales agency, the average less-trained producer made it to that level after their sixth film. The more-trained producer did it after their second film. The finance teams at talent agencies only open their doors for producers when there is a real chance that the agency's clients will get a role in the film. This is yet another indication that more-trained producers attract stars faster.

To put a bow on all of this, my evidence suggests that more-trained producers make bigger films and get to the more-sophisticated parts of the film finance system faster than their less-trained counterparts. If you want to maximize your potential as a producer, I recommend that you work for someone else until you are well-trained.

* * *

I will pause to remind you that I am drawing conclusions based on statistics. The numbers say that, typically, one career path appears superior to the other. Buried within those digits is a reality that some folks did not work a long time for someone else, and still built amazing careers. For instance, Charlize Theron's producing partner, A.J. Dix, only spent four years after college at New Line before his bosses greenlit his first film. Amazing talents like Mr. Dix and many others get by without putting in eight or more years. (Granted, he works so hard, Mr. Dix might have done eight years-worth of work in his brief tenure at New Line.)

There are also people like Thomas Mahoney, producer of 2021 Sundance selection, *Wild Indian*. Mr. Mahoney completed his studies at the American Film Institute, then went straight to producing his first film, *Prototype*. Unprompted, he told me, "I don't like to work for other people." *Sleight* producer Eric Fleischman used almost the exact same words. I get that. I don't like to work for other people either. If I must confess, I have animosity towards anyone with power over me, even if they're incredibly nice and helpful. That's why I am a professor, where I essentially have no boss. (Although, I spent about nine years working or attending grad school first.) If you feel that way too, then decide if you want to be miserable for years working for other people, or be happy working for yourself.

Take this as guidance, not a rule. If you want to improve your chances of building a successful producing career, work for someone else. Or, in finance terms, if you want to reduce your career risk, find a great boss.

* * *

Jason Blum is one of the most successful producers of the last 20 years. He made a fortune on *Paranormal Activity*, and then grew that fortune by producing nearly 200 other film & TV titles through his Blumhouse Productions banner, including *Get Out*, *The Purge*, and *Insidious*. For every dollar spent on production, Blumhouse films generate an average of $10 at the box office globally. No one in the history of film has consistently generated the financial success of Blumhouse.

Like all of us, Mr. Blum didn't start out successful. The first movie he tried to make was 1995's *Kicking and Screaming*. Through a family connection, Mr. Blum was able to get Steve Martin to read the script. While Mr. Martin was not willing to act in the movie, he wrote a very nice letter on his own stationery about how much he liked the script. Mr. Blum attached that letter to the cover of every script he sent out thereafter, to give credibility to the project. Soon enough, they had their cast and their financing, and the film got made.

This is a great lesson in the power of credibility. Mr. Martin's letter made Mr. Blum's script credible in the eyes of anyone who received it. In a world with so many producers trying to break in, anything that you can do to make yourself more credible helps. If you do not personally know Steve Martin or someone of similar stature who can vouch for you, then good work experience that builds skills and connections is an important source of credibility for financiers.

In documentary filmmaking, investors are concerned with both your professional credibility and the credibility of your access. For instance, Doug Pray went to capture the Seattle music scene in 1992, at a time that he says, "everybody was going to Seattle with cameras." In order to be credible to potential investors, he needed to show that he had access to the musicians that were refusing to be interviewed for other projects. Luckily, he did have access. One of his good friends from college, a member of a local band called the "Young Fresh Fellows," vouched for Mr. Pray in the right circles. Before long, he had a list of 30 interview subjects that he could send out to convince potential investors that he had access. It took about four years to wrap, but his completed film, *Hype*, stood out amongst the crowd of Seattle grunge docs, and earned a place at Sundance followed by a theatrical release.

Mr. Pray will tell you to this day that "access is the most important thing to gain momentum for fundraising." In narrative, the movie stars are your stars, and having access to them is important for your financiers. Similarly, in docs, the subjects are your stars, and having access to them will make your film viable. As you gain more and more access, your potential investors will show more and more interest in your film. That access comes in part through credibility, like Steve Martin's letter on Jason Blum's script. Some people are born with those links, but most need to work hard and network like crazy over many years to make connections that provide access.

Takeaways

- Producers with more work experience prior to producing their first movie end up with more impactful careers than those with less work experience.
- Working for someone else early in your career gives you skills, connections, and credibility.
- There is no optimal work experience for producers. Build a skill stack that helps you stand out from the crowd.

Notes

1 This footnote may be too technical, but I love this story. One of his recent films was pitched to investors with a US-dollar budget, even though it would be shot in South Africa. To complicate matters more, the lead investor would eventually contribute cash in British pounds. Mr. Goodman-Bhyat was savvy enough to lock the exchange rates through a series of forward transactions on the financial markets. Had he not done so, the currency fluctuations would have put him $1 million away from completing the film by the time they were ready to shoot. If you are in a similar position someday, there are banks and currency exchange companies who can help you lock currencies so your budget is safe too.
2 The medians are much lower than the average because of some big homeruns. Amongst the less-trained, the lifetime box office *average* is $46 million, while it is $121 million amongst the more-trained.
3 This analysis uses a statistical technique called ordinary least squares regression. The difference in votes is significant at the 1% level.

14 People Matter

> It's interdependent film, not independent film.
> – Mike Gabrawy, producer

> Have a ton of relationships, and gain a ton of perspective from those relationships.
> – Stephen Gibler, producer

One of the best pieces of advice that I ever got in my career was to "always work with the best partners." (Ironically, the person who gave me that advice went to prison for defrauding retirees. I wish he had taken his own advice.) As a finance professor, the best partners are the smartest, the hardest working, and the most creative professors working in the same area of research. My partners have all been deliberately chosen, and all helped me take an idea and craft it into a finished work with an audience. If not for them, I would not have been given the gift of tenure, and I would not be writing this book today. The people that I chose to work with are the foundation of my career success.

Whenever you are starting a project, be very picky about the financiers and other partners you work with. At that moment, at inception, you get to choose the partners who will be by your side through thick and thin. Do not pick the people who are most convenient. Spend time, a lot of time, considering who will be the best co-pilot on your mission. Seek them out, ask the right questions to make sure that you will be able to work together and negotiate your differences, and convince them to be part of your team only if the fit is right.

Producers generally carry three overlapping philosophies about the types of people that they want working on their films. The first is highlighted by producer Peter Phok, who encourages you to "bring in partners who believe in the project." Tom McNulty, producer of *The Spectacular Now*, extends that advice to recommend that you "find people who are passionate about the film and willing to hustle and/or cut their fees." The second prevalent philosophy that others stressed is

DOI: 10.4324/9781003363446-18

the importance of working with the best people, like the advice that I was given early in my career. The third – no jerks. In a perfect world, the best people will also be passionate about your film, willing to hustle, willing to cut their fees to get it made, and not be difficult to work with.

Now and for the rest of your career, you will need to find folks with passion, hustle, amazing skillsets, decency, and money to fill the various roles on your films. As *The Tale* producer, Mynette Louie professes, "you have to be outgoing and meet people." Take every opportunity that you can to get to know people who are or might want to be involved in the process of making movies. But it goes beyond that. Writer and producer Toby Halbrooks observes that successful filmmakers are "good at having relationships without burning bridges." His personal philosophy – which may be the most charming thing anyone has said to me in years – is to try to be "base-level decent."

This chapter offers producers' thoughts on where to meet the investors and collaborators needed to get your project finished. There is so much wisdom in these pages for you to enjoy.

Film School and Business School

> You don't have to be a genius, just be a people person.
> – Greg Lauritano, producer

Film school holds tremendous value as a place to begin building your professional network. Get to know as many of your classmates as possible, and help as many as possible. One of my interviewees produced six senior projects in his final year of film school, both so he had a lot of experience when he graduated, and so he could show many of his classmates that he was skilled. Immediately upon graduation, he got a chance to produce his first feature. It would be directed by a classmate, who had already raised six figures from her family and friends.

Do not rule out business school. Producing is a business, and knowing how businesses work will give you an advantage over producers who do not. Many of my interview subjects went through a business program, either as an undergraduate or an MBA student. There are new entertainment-focused graduate business programs around the world too. All of these provide a path to learning business fundamentals and meeting new people. Several of my interview subjects were able to raise money from their business school classmates, so you may find that benefit too.

Be kind to all of your classmates. Lots of people are still growing up in college, and just need a few more years to mature. Some are dealing with family problems, others with yet-to-be-diagnosed medical problems, and many need more time to find themselves. (I do not think I was a particularly decent person until I was about 30 years old.) When they do find their adult selves, they will appreciate your compassion and tolerance.

Do not just limit your networking to your classmates. Producer Scott Veltri recommends that you "use your alumni network." Graduates of your school are more likely to help you than a random person off the street. Meet your professors, go to their office hours, and make sure they know what you want to accomplish in your career. They know lots of people, and can connect you with alumni who might be able to help your career.

On the Job

> Work hard – people will notice.
> – Andrew Harvey, producer

Most people in the entertainment business are trying to do much, much more with their career. So many of the folks that you meet in the office or on set are hoping to write, produce, direct, or star in a movie someday. Aspirations run thick in this business. If you find the right, motivated peer group, you will all go far together. Producer Chuck West advises you to, "put your resources together and make yourself more powerful."

Nicholas Tabarrok suggests that you invite every assistant that you talk to out to coffee or lunch. In most entry-level jobs in the entertainment industry, you will meet lots of assistants. Many of them will be powerful someday – the heads of the major agencies almost all started out in the mail room and assistant desk at the beginning of their careers – and you will gain a lot of access by knowing them when they were young.

Do not discount the value of young people in the film industry, especially your co-workers. They will be in charge in just a few years, and it is much easier to get to know them now when their calendars are not full. Naomi Despres, producer of *Kill the Messenger*, will tell you that "the relationships from your first jobs are the most important in your career." Be sure to hang out with your coworkers outside of the workplace to get to know each other better. Who knows – that person in the mailroom might be working on the perfect script for your next film.

Film Markets, Festivals, and Premieres

> Find a support network of peers at film festivals.
> – Janet Yang, producer and president of the Academy of Motion Picture Arts and Sciences

If you have not yet met my colleague and *I, Tonya* executive producer Rosanne Korenberg, I hope you get to someday. She is a real treasure, and a wonderful member of the independent filmmaking community. Ms. Korenberg started her career like you, trying to figure out how to go from the ground floor to being a successful producer. She built her career by attending as many film markets and festivals as possible (at her employer's expense) and meeting as many people as possible. Through that experience, she had a huge network at her disposal when she was ready to make her first feature on her own.

Ms. Korenberg and so many other producers will tell you the importance of attending film markets and festivals, especially early in your career. As the title of this chapter says, People Matter, and there is no better place to meet the kind of people who will help your career than at festivals. Producers go to festivals, to see their films play before an audience, to meet with sales agents and distributors, and to reconnect with old friends. Directors and writers go, to try to find collaborators for their next project. Equity investors go, to live the Hollywood dream and see their movie on the big screen. Film commissioners, lenders, lawyers, consultants, and aspiring filmmakers of all stripes go too. There is no better place to meet a ton of people who might want to work with you someday.

While at the festival, make every effort to get to know all of the people involved in organizing it. They are vital to the world of independent film, and more importantly, might be considering your entry someday. Producer Josh Penn says that meeting them once "won't get you into a festival, but knowing people gets you out of the middle of the pack and in consideration."

There are project markets attached to some of the film festivals, which are designed to get producers with interesting scripts in front of co-producers, investors, sales agents, and distributors. These project markets are great ways to meet the right types of people to get your film off the ground, if you can get in. CineMart at the International Film Festival Rotterdam (IFFR) claims to be the first platform of its kind, and other project markets have emerged too in recent years. They grew out of organizations including Sundance (called Catalyst), the European Film Market (Berlinale Co-Production Market), Film Independent (Fast Track), and The Gotham Film and Media Institute (Gotham Week Project Market). These are all highly selective and have a rigorous application process. The smallest, Fast Track, only takes 15 projects per year. The Berlinale Co-Production Market is the biggest, but caps out at just 25 scripts. Most do not charge a fee for submitting a script, so at least you can try to get in for free.

You do not actually have to buy a ticket to benefit from the networking around film events. If you go to the bars and coffee shops around South by Southwest, Sundance, TIFF, or any other large film festival, you will meet people who are there to get movies made and distributed. While you are there, find out what other parties people are going to, and figure out if you can get in to those too. From experience, I can tell you that the finance parties are not wild, but the people are friendly and you'll meet a ton of lenders and lawyers who may be able to help get your film made someday.

Along similar lines, be sure to hold premieres for all of your finished projects, and make them as big as possible. That is how *April 29, 1992* producer Maurice Fadida really got his start. He and a few buddies made a series called *Borderline* on their own. Each of them would work a day job for a few weeks and save a few bucks, and then get together and shoot some scenes. It took them 18 months of working, saving, and shooting, but they finally got all six episodes wrapped and distributed on Amazon Prime. Even though they were practically broke, they were able to convince a friend to let them use a screen at the Chinese Theater for a premiere. They made the premiere as big as possible, and invited everyone that they hoped to work with someday. Through that event, a financier was convinced that Mr. Fadida could produce features, and committed to a sizable investment in his next film.

The *Borderline* premiere is definitely not the only time that young producers have used such an event to get buy-in on their next project. It happens a lot. If you can produce a show AND you can produce a successful premiere on a shoestring budget, then you have proven that you have the chops to produce a feature. Leverage your connections and use your premiere as a tool to show people how much you have accomplished. It will open doors for you.

* * *

Producer Jeff Sackman tells a heartbreaking story about a festival premier gone wrong. Prior to the screening, he had a $5 million offer on the table for U.S., U.K., and Australian distribution rights for one of his completed projects. At that price, all of his investors would have been repaid, and then some. The distributor/buyer really wanted to seal the deal before his competitors watched the premier at the festival. Wanting to keep his options open, Mr. Sackman said "maybe."

The premier did not goes as planned. In Mr. Sackman's own words, "It was possibly the worst screening ever. Bad. Flat. People walking out." In the end, the original distributor reduced his offer to $2.75 million for U.S. rights only, and Mr. Sackman will tell you he was very fortunate to get that price. In his experience, he finds that "in almost every situation, the first offer turns out to be the best offer."

Local Filmmaker Events

> Find someone who is a great filmmaker, and make things happen for them.
>
> – Greg Lauritano, producer

Whether with SFFilm in the Bay Area, DOC NYC, or something run by a local film commission, there are lots of functions each year designed to get filmmakers together. Often, they work. Mike Gabrawy was consulting for Film Independent back in the late 1990s, with access to their events. At one such gathering, he met the person who would become the key equity investor for one of his first feature films, *All You Need*. In order for that serendipitous meeting to occur, Mr. Gabrawy first had to show up and shake some hands.

Networking events are really scary. You will walk into a room full of people seemingly having fun, intense, lively conversations, and it will be intimidating. Here is what you need to bring to make it successful:

1. A smile
2. The willingness to ask, "Can I join you?"

That's it. As long as you show up prepared to be friendly and ask to be included, you will meet people who may be able to help you. You'll almost certainly be able to help them too. I am a firm believer that everybody has a way to add value to a relationship, and so it is really important that you do not discount your own worth, and search for ways that you can support the people that you meet.

Notice that I did not have friends on that list of things to bring to a networking event. I strongly believe in the value of going alone. If you go with friends, you will meet fewer people and give yourself less time to introduce yourself and your interests to the people in the room.

Also, here's a secret about networking events. That fun, intense, lively atmosphere that you first walk into is not at all what it seems. It looks like groups of friends out having a good time. In reality, it is groups of strangers trying hard to be pleasant and fun with one another. Most walked into the event alone, and most are there with the intention of making new connections.

That's why asking the question, "Can I join you?" is so effective. Nine times out of ten, the group that you just walked up to is excited to meet you and learn about you. On rare occasions, you will run into folks who are having an exclusive conversation, and you will be politely encouraged to mingle elsewhere, but most of the time, you will be welcomed into the conversation.

Your goal in these conversations is to find something that you and another person have in common. Everyone in the room has a passion for filmmaking, so it needs to be different than that. You might connect over hometowns, other jobs, or hobbies (I can talk to my fellow surfers in the room all night). Sometimes, you will just find people with whom you have compatible personalities. Your connection, whatever it is, is the gateway to building a professional relationship.

Breakfasts, Lunches, and Happy Hours

> When you find someone who likes you, pay attention to them.
> – Clay Pecorin, producer

In every city around the world, aspiring filmmakers host formal and informal networking events. Take advantage. If there isn't one close to you, make one. When only two people show up the first week, be persistent and try again. (All successful independent filmmakers are persistent – this may be your first test.)

Despite all of the advice in the prior sections, Zaheer Goodman-Bhyat advises young filmmakers to go to lunches, not parties. His feeling is that parties are for schmoozing, while lunches are a chance to have deeper, quieter conversations. I understand that viewpoint, and, frankly, prefer breakfasts and lunches too. Maybe the most important thing is to socialize the way that makes you comfortable.

Churches and Charities

Churches and charities draw two constituencies that are critical for filmmakers: donors and passionate advocates. Of the two, the passionate advocates may be more valuable. In building your pitch and your business plan, being able to point to a built-in audience is a great asset. These volunteers will be the first to see your film when it is released. They are going to spread the word about it, and make sure others watch it too. They want your film to be a success, and will do their part to make sure it is.

The advice that producer Todd Burns gives to young filmmakers is that, "there has to be meaning and purpose to what you do." Over his lifetime, Mr. Burns has started dozens of nonprofit organizations, and occasionally collaborates with those nonprofits to make a documentary to help shine light on the issue.

If you belong to a religious congregation, be sure to let every single one of your fellow worshippers know about your project, especially if religious or moral themes are baked into your story. Some equity investors are motivated by making a social impact. If your movie allows people in your congregation to feel like they are sharing a valuable moral lesson on the big screen, then they are more likely to become investors.

Grocery Stores

> Talk to anyone. Talk to people in your town, build your network, and see if you can find that person who can write that check.
> – Matthew Parker, producer

I say that grocery stores are an important place to meet people only somewhat facetiously, because I have been told about three features that found financing in the line at the checkout. Once your pitch is rock solid, I guess maybe you should shop where the people with money shop, and be prepared to deliver that pitch to everyone in line at the checkout?

Nonetheless, the point stands that you should always be ready to deliver your elevator pitch to everyone you meet, just in case they are the one YES you need to get your film made. The financiers who will provide funding for your first film are often Average Jane on the street. They are everywhere, and seemingly nowhere.

Nonspecific Networking and Angel Investor Events

This will be my one contrary bullet in this chapter. I do not encourage you to attend networking and angel investor events that are not specific to film. None of the producers that I talked to mentioned ever meeting an investor at such an event. Triple-threat producer/writer/director Jon Keeyes is a charming, charismatic presence in any room. He is the kind of person who would shine at a networking event if anyone did. Yet, even Mr. Keeyes noted that he attended many such events around his home in Texas, and never found a good source of funding at any of them.

All of Mr. Keeyes' investors have been introduced to him by family, friends, or his other investors. If your family is big, that is a big help. If not, then make sure you build lots of friendships that you can rely on in the years to come.

* * *

You will need to continue meeting people for the rest of your career in order to find investors and get your movie made. This chapter offers some of the best paths that successful producers have used to find new collaborators. You do not need to use all of them, but you must be persistent about meeting new people for years to come if you want to sustain your career.

15 Pipelines Matter

> Shoot, I have to do this again!
> – Clark Peterson, producer

> There was tons of stuff that failed to get off the ground.
> – Naomi Despres, producer

Every movie that gets made is a little miracle. There is so much that can go wrong along the way to derail a film. You may not be able to get the rights. Even if you get the rights, you may not be able to get the actors you need. Even if you get the actors, you may not be able to get the financing. Even if you get the financing, you may not be able to get everyone together at the same time to shoot (and then your financier will drop out). Even if you get everyone together at the same time to shoot, your lead actor may be injured or otherwise unable to complete their scenes. Even if you make it through principal photography, you may not have the money to complete post-production. Even if you complete post-production, you may not be able to find distribution. Even if you find distribution, your distributor may go belly-up right before your film is supposed to be released (right, Weinstein Company, Relativity Media, and Global Road). Even if your film gets released, your distributor may never pay you.

There are so many risks along the way!

The way that successful producers and movie studios manage these risks is by keeping many films at various stages of production at all times, otherwise known as a pipeline. Producer Josh Penn highlights the need for a pipeline as he talks about *Beasts of the Southern Wild*. From the start of production through its amazing run at the Oscars, he said, "I had only thought of 'Beasts' for so long." As calls started coming in from people who wanted to work with him on his next project, Mr. Penn will concede that he "didn't have anything else lined up." His cupboard was bare, and he will tell you that it was a missed opportunity. Having different projects in your pipeline as you develop in your career is critical to your success.

We all have our own tastes, but the broader variety of projects that you can have in your pipeline, the better. Society's tastes in films can change surprisingly quickly – think about how tastes changed at the last minute because of terrorist acts, gun violence, #MeToo, Black Lives Matter, and COVID. If you have variety in your pipeline, you will increase your chances of having a project that meets the current needs of society, whatever they may be.

The reality is that you will get turned down at most pitch meetings. I had a wonderful, candid conversation about this very topic with the hard-working Lauren Bixby, Senior Vice President of Acquisitions and Co-Productions at Lionsgate. Ms. Bixby explained that she likes to source some of her projects from a network of reliable producers, who are honest and take feedback well. By her estimates, she will tell those preferred business partners seven NOs for every one YES. Even the most successful producers with deep connections to the studios get turned down far more than you might expect. According to Ms. Bixby, the reason they get another shot with her team is because "they take the NO well, and have other ideas how to bounce back." In other words, they have a thick skin and a pipeline that makes each rejection less painful.

Producer Naomi Despres will tell you about the importance of developing a thick skin, so you can take the NO well. When I spoke to her, she said, "NOs used to get me down, and now it's just like water off my back." To develop a thick skin, you need to be told NO a lot. That will be stressful, but it is a necessary part of becoming a successful producer.

You can use short films to increase the volume of your pipeline. So, so many of the producers that contributed to this book recommend filming shorts on your phone as often as possible. Proof of concept goes a long way in generating interest for larger projects. Shorts are a great mechanism for establishing tone and visual language as you sell your pitch. Filming lots of low budget shorts with your friends gives you lots of chances to make a hit. Most may end up missing, never to be seen again, but in the process, two good things can result. First, you will build your skillset managing the filmmaking process. Second, you may actually make something good that gets seen and serves as a calling card to get you a bigger opportunity.

Maybe an even more important reason to have a pipeline is the famous chicken-and-egg problem in film finance. It is difficult to find financing without having talent attached. It is also difficult to get talent attached without having financing in place. Matthew Rhodes, president of the financing and production company, The Hideaway Entertainment, figured out a solution: find someone who loves the film as much as you. If that person is an actor who really wants the part, then they will lend their name to your pitch and meet with potential investors with you. On the flip side, if you do not have actors attached yet, but you found a financier who loves the story and must see it get made, then they will work with you to attract talent. Either way, the poultry problem can only ever be solved by finding partners who love the film, and that is as much true for your first film as your 20th. Your job as a producer will always be finding someone to commit first, to solve the chicken-and-egg problem.

Thomas Mahoney, producer of *The Girl in the Photographs*, wisely told me that, "your next movie will not be what you think your next movie will be." His statement is a reflection of the fact that films come together serendipitously, as producers find the right partners. If you always have several projects in your pipeline, you give yourself more chances to find a match to solve the chicken-and-egg problem. Robust pipelines are essential to building a successful career.

Do not try to build a pipeline of features on your own. It is work that must be done with partners. If you do not have the people yet to help you build a full slate, then refer back to Chapter 14. You will need to meet people to help you grow your pipeline, and keep meeting people to sustain it.

16 Luck Matters

> Sometimes, you just get lucky.
>
> – Gill Holland, producer

Producer Clark Peterson was kind enough to tell me the story of how *Monster* got distributed back in 2003. You remember *Monster*, right? The movie that launched *Wonder Woman* director Patty Jenkins' career and won Charlize Theron the Best Leading Actress Academy Award.

It turns out, *Monster* was independently financed and produced without any domestic distribution in place. The filmmakers had no means to get it to American viewers and generate money to repay their investors once it was done. It was made on spec. The producers brought a VHS copy to every major studio and allowed the acquisitions executives to see Charlize Theron's Oscar-winning performance. They watched the whole film. They saw it with their own eyes, completed, and in all its glory.

There obviously should have been a bidding war, but something strange happened. Every single studio – passed – on the chance to distribute *Monster*. Every single one. Credible estimates indicate that the producers had just spent $5 million, but no studio was interested in distributing their finished film in the United States.

The only company who was open to signing a contract to get the movie to American viewers was the nation's leading video rental chain at the time, Blockbuster Video. Blockbuster wanted exclusive rental rights, and was willing to pay for them. Luckily, Blockbuster was savvy enough to know that video renters would be more excited to see the film if it had the prestige of a theatrical run before being available on video. After all, theatrical runs come with marketing campaigns, which bring awareness through billboards, newspaper & radio ads, and listings in the weekend box office numbers. They also bring critical reviews and the prospects of an Oscar nomination. Movies are not inherently prestigious in the eyes of the public just because they play in theaters, but because of all of the attention that comes with the movie playing in a theater.

DOI: 10.4324/9781003363446-20

Blockbuster committed to a small theatrical marketing campaign before the video release, but had no idea what they were getting into. In the first week, *Monster* was on four screens nationwide, and the cost of advertising was pretty small. As more and more newspapers published praise-filled reviews and word of mouth spread, the release quickly expanded to 14 screens, then 82. Before Blockbuster knew what was happening, *Monster* was a top-five film on 1,093 screens. Each screen added more copies of the physical films (at about $1,500 each, or over $1.6 million for all 1,093 screens), more newspaper ads, and more movie theater posters. Blockbuster could have said NO to all that spending, but recognized the value it would bring when the video finally hit their shelves exclusively, so they kept spending. They wrote checks weekly to cover the added costs. In the end, the nation's leading video rental chain spent over $10 million on a theatrical campaign.

This story is filled with some really good luck in that all of the elements came together: Charlize Theron put in an incredible performance and won an Oscar, first-time director Patty Jenkins masterfully executed the story, and Blockbuster Video said YES and then kept saying YES. Those outcomes, all of that good luck, could only happen because of the producers' combined skillsets, hard work, and good connections.

Producers fell into two camps when I asked them about the luck in their career. On one hand, there are those like Maurice Fadida, who told me, "I don't get lucky, I get prepared." Quite a few very successful producers do not attribute anything to luck, and insist that all of their success is due to hard work and meticulous planning. On the other hand, there are producers, when asked about the luckiest thing that happened in their career, they respond "the whole thing." So many are still gobsmacked that they get to make movies for a living, and consider every moment of their careers to be one giant stroke of luck.

By the way, the person who said "the whole thing" was good luck was also Maurice Fadida. While that strikes as a contradiction to his action hero-like, "I don't get lucky, I get prepared" quote at first, both can be true. Mr. Fadida and others must plan for every possible contingency, so that when fortune or misfortune happens, they have a way forward already in place.

Producer A.J. Dix told me that "you can't manufacture good luck, but you can improve the chances." The best way to improve your chances of seizing upon good luck is with the experience, people, and pipelines that were discussed in the previous three chapters. These three elements are cumulative, they feed each other. On the job training gives you connections, tools, resources, and wisdom that you can bring into play once luck strikes you. With that experience, you will know what to do when you get that first YES. To get to a YES, it will help to have a pipeline of projects so you have the right story ready to go when you get that lucky meeting with the right talent and financiers. To get from script to screen, you will need to know great people, who can help turn the vision into reality.

    I hope that good luck happens to you a lot in your career. More importantly, I hope that you are prepared for luck to happen to you.

17 Many Other Things Matter Too

Successful producers are bursting with wisdom. Their invaluable financial advice that did not fit neatly into another chapter is presented in these brief sections.

Pitches Matter

> You are the best representative for your project.
> – Janet Yang, producer and president of the Academy of Motion Picture Arts and Sciences

This is far from a book about how to deliver the perfect pitch, but your pitch is an essential tool for raising money.

To be clear here, there are two types of pitches in the film world: creative pitches and investor pitches. In the creative pitch, you are presenting the story and hoping other creatives find it exciting. You'll use this pitch to get creatives, talent agents, sales agents, and managers on board.

The other type of pitch is the investor pitch, and the audience is anyone who might contribute equity to your film. It needs to begin with the business opportunity for the investor, and include some elements of your creative pitch, all within 30 seconds. While an investor is interested in the story, they are really interested in what they will get out of the investment. Talk about social impact, red carpet premieres, or anything else of value that you plan to give your investor. And it needs to be exciting!

It is your job to practice your investor pitch as much as possible, on anyone who will listen, even your hamster. Aim to make it more exciting every time you deliver it. Make sure that everyone you meet hears the pitch for your film. I mean everyone. Tell your dentist while trapped in their chair. Tell the woman sitting at the car wash. Tell the person hurriedly taking your picture at the DMV. It should feel a little like the movie *Groundhog Day*, in that you will repeat your pitch over and over. Each time you say it, you will learn how to deliver it a little better (or realize that you hit a dead-end and need to start over), until you finally get your YES.

DOI: 10.4324/9781003363446-21

When someone is receptive to your pitch, ask how you can send them your business plan. Deliver the copy to them within 24 hours, while their curiosity is still piqued. Follow up in a week if you haven't heard back.

If you do not have a business plan yet, it is time to get started on one. I like Louise Levison's book, *Filmmakers and Financing* as a starting place to writing a business plan for your movie.

There are two important adjustments to her book that I recommend. First, include your film's budget. Investors need to know how much it will cost to make your film. They will use that information to figure out how much cash they need to contribute. If you don't include a budget, you may be creating the impression that you're not very professional and you try to cut corners. Neither of those attributes are very appealing to a savvy investor. Work with a line producer to get your budget nailed down.

Second, show the First Law of Film Finance (that the market value must be bigger than the financing plan, and the financing plan must be bigger than the budget) to your investors. Make a good-faith estimate of the market value of the film, and show as much of the financing plan as possible. If you expect to use tax incentives or other soft money, include that in your financing plan. Make sure this is early in your business plan. Most potential investors will care more about the financial success of the film than the key plot points.

If possible, follow up with a meeting with any potential investor to listen to their aspirations and see if you can help them meet their goals. Remember, this isn't just about you finding money for your film, it's also about them finding the right person to invest in. If you talk instead of listening in that meeting, you will probably miss a chance to learn something important.

Even with a perfect pitch, solid business plan, and an amazing follow-up meeting, there is a good chance that they will give you a "no." Most investors say no. Do not burn that bridge. Be gracious for their consideration, and they may be a yes on your next film.

Good Attorneys Matter

> My left hand is a lawyer and my right hand is a lawyer.
> – Matthew Rhodes, producer

If you did not notice, several times throughout this book, I suggested that you hire a good attorney (and I was not compensated for saying that). This advice comes from me and from so many of the people that I spoke with. Financier Thomas Mann advised me to bold and underline all of the parts about hiring a good attorney.

Good lawyers are expensive, and for a reason. They will save you so much time and so much money as you are trying to build your career. I teach from real lawsuits filed in real courts in my Entertainment Finance course at Loyola Marymount University, and I see some of the silly mistakes that sloppy attorneys make in their contracts. Entertainment law is its own thing. Do not hire your cousin, the real estate lawyer, to do the job for you. Do not hire the cheap paralegal that no one has ever heard of. Get recommendations from other producers, and spend the money.

If you cannot afford a good entertainment attorney, you are not ready to produce a feature yet. Keep working, growing your skillset, building your connections, and saving money until you can afford one.

Youth Matters

> Take risks while you're young.
>
> – Stu Pollard, producer

The clock is ticking. The reality is that you have just a few years to establish your career before you are too late. Before long, you will have social pressures to "get a real job" and earn a real paycheck. Before long, you might have a partner and kids and far less free time. Before long, you will be worn out and looking for something more stable. Before long, you will be out of touch with what is cool. Before long, your health will not be what it was in your 20s.

Several producers spoke to the virtues of being underpaid when you are young. *The Green Knight* producer Toby Halbrooks insists that filmmaking is really a competition of "who can live at their grandmother's house the longest." Similarly, Gill Holland will advise you that "the longer you can afford to be broke, the higher your chances of success." If you can tolerate a bit of poverty when you are young, it may help your career.

Producer Scott Veltri urges you to "start as soon as you can." Take advantage of your youthfulness now. Work really hard. Meet everyone that you can at as many parties and happy hours as you can access.[1] Take as many weekend and evening classes as possible, in person or online, and get to know all of the people in the room with you. Cram every day like you have a test tomorrow.

One particularly impactful way to take advantage of your youthfulness is to find mentors who love to help the next generation, and nurture mutually-beneficial relationships with them. Lots of older, well-connected people are full of wisdom and just want some young sponge to soak it up in a no-strings attached connection. This is not weird or creepy – it is human nature. Human children expect to learn.

To feed that expectation, human adults expect to teach. It is wired in our DNA, and essential to our survival as a species. Use that to your advantage. Let the elder generation teach you and guide you, and see where those connections take you.

The way that I encourage my students to find these relationships is by first asking for an informational interview with the potential mentor. Your goal in this initial meeting is just to learn about them and their career. If it clicks, ask for a second meeting in a few months to get more of their advice and wisdom. If that goes well, ask for another. By the time you get that third meeting, they will be your mentor, even without you formally asking.

You are far more likely to get that first meeting if you are introduced to your potential mentor by a contact who already knows them. This is often called a warm introduction (versus a cold call).[2] The important thing about warm introductions is to make them as easy as possible on your contacts who are offering you the favor. First write a thoughtful email to your contact explaining who you want to meet and why you want to meet them. From there, it will be very easy for your contact to just forward along your email, suggesting that your potential mentor meet with you.

Banking and Accounting Matter

> Have all of the money in the bank.
>
> – Matthew Parker, producer

On an independent production in 2021, a hacker broke into a producer's email account. The perpetrator communicated to the producing team that the Bank of America account number had changed, and the $500,000+ from the equity financier was supposed to go to a new account at Bank of America. Within a day, the money was in the hacker's account.

The producer who told me this story admitted that all of the right people were copied on the email chain, "but they changed a letter in your email address, so I can see that this guy's copied and that guy's copied and it looked normal," but none of the right people actually saw that the hack was occurring because the email addresses were intentionally wrong.

A few hours after the deposit was made, one of the producers discovered something was amiss, and tried to stop the payment. They were told that the money was already sent, but the bank immediately froze the hacker's account before the funds could be withdrawn. If the bank had returned the money quickly, they could all laugh about it and go on making their movie. Instead bank investigators spent four weeks making sure that they were giving this six-figure chunk of cash to the right party.

For many independent productions, not having the cash in the bank account at the start of shooting would be the event that causes the whole film to collapse. Luckily, this was a very experienced production team that was able to hold the film together. The producers missed payroll payments and ran into other problems in those four weeks, but the film got shot.

In order for your film to get finished and your investors to get repaid, you need to keep careful watch over your cash. Be careful to hire a reputable accountant who knows the banking side of the business well, and is familiar with the many ways that people steal from independent productions. They will be worth every penny you pay them (unless they're the one stealing your money, which sometimes happens too).

Los Angeles Matters

> Everything leads in the end to Los Angeles.
> – Robbert Aarts, Co-CEO of Fintage House

I mentioned in the beginning of this book that, despite the fact that only about one-fifth of the producers in the sample are from the Greater Los Angeles, California metropolitan area (LA), 77% indicate that they are working out of LA now. With so many studios, talent agencies, sales agencies, distributors, producers, directors, and financiers running their businesses out of LA, it is the easiest place to participate in the industry. That body of talent makes Southern California a great place to meet people with similar or complementary career aspirations. Many producers also earn income with jobs related to the movie business, such as teaching courses at film schools, directing television commercials or music videos, line producing, and providing consulting services. Therefore, working out of LA provides additional opportunities to earn an income and connect with other professionals.

Looking at the statistics, we can see evidence that people working in LA achieved even more career success than those working from other locations. The lifetime box office earned by those in LA is nearly four times that earned by outsiders. Angelenos' films also earned nearly twice as many votes on IMDB as those working from outside LA. The evidence suggests that the synergies from working in LA are real.

Cybill Lui Eppich, producer of *The Silencing*, tried to build a career in New York before moving to Los Angeles. "You can't do it in New

York," she told me. "What you'll learn in a week in LA will take you months in New York."

Control Maybe Does Not Matter

Many young producers are concerned about having control over their project. They want to make sure that it fits their vision, is cast the way they want, shot the way they want, and distributed the way they want. They do not want someone else telling them how to do their job or taking away their authority. By working hard to control the project, they shut out partners who could help get the film financed and finished, and it never gets made.

Sisters producer Cathy Gesualdo put it best when she said, "Control over what? The director? The actors? The weather? Making a movie is about giving up control to a team and to forces beyond your control."

You will give up control of some things that are important to you in order to get your film made. Compromise is a necessary part of working with other people, and your film is going to take the work of lots of other people to get made. If all goes well, those compromises will make your finished movie better, not worse.

When you give up some of your control to another producer, it is critical that you do your homework and make sure that person is going to be a good partner. Naomi Despres advises that, "it is not worth it to make the film with partners who are going to ride roughshod over you and not share the same vision." It would be wise to talk to their former producing partners and see what their experiences were like. It would also be wise to come to an agreement about who is in control of what pieces of the project. Just remember, there are people in any industry who get to the tops of their careers by stepping on the backs of others. A few famous producers have been in the news in recent years who fit that description.

I spoke with one producer who lost control of his second movie and its finances, when a more senior producer came on board with a famous athlete as the lead equity investor. The film recouped, but this individual was never paid his producing fees or participations. After winning a lawsuit and a court order to pay against the senior producer, he still has not received payment, more than 15 years after the film's release. Producers like this are happy to share their experiences working with their former producing partners, so that the same thing does not happen to someone else.

Always use a collection account manager, like Fintage or Freeway. Do not be vague about which producer gets what share of the cash flows. Work with an attorney to properly write an agreement to share any producers' fees or profits. Also be sure there is an understanding about who controls the bank account.

Your Stress Tolerance Matters

> There are a whole lot easier ways to make a living. There are a lot easier ways to make money.
>
> – Clark Peterson, producer

I am amazed by the amount of stress that these producers endured in nearly every interview that I conducted. Movies falling apart at the last minute. Crews walking off set. Talent behaving irrationally. All while working exhausting days during film shoots. To be a successful producer, you will have to thrive under stress. When everything seems like it is going wrong, director and producer Alessandra Pasquino said, "no matter who is freaking out or why they're freaking out, we have to land the plane." Her method for coping with stress is to break things down into small pieces, and then attack the small pieces. In Ms. Pasquino's words, "Something goes wrong all the time. As long as no one dies, it's ok."

Maximilian Leo, producer of *7500*, is still blown away by the strange fact that "you are competing with your idols from day one." That's crazy! That does not happen in most businesses. Every producer mentioned in this book is effectively your competition. They are trying to beat you to the best stories, the best talent, and the best sources of financing. Yet, you have a chance. You bring new skills, new awareness of emerging technologies, new taste in stories, and new energy. You can compete, but it will be stressful.

Janet Yang, president of the Academy of Motion Picture Arts and Sciences, explained to me that the stress of producing is easier to manage "if you love to solve problems and have a thick skin." Every movie is just a series of problems that need to be solved. To the extent that you get deep satisfaction from finding a resolution and seeing the finished project, then this is a great business for you.

The good thing about being a producer is that you at least get to decide what you work on, and projects that are meaningful to you make the stress more tolerable. Documentarian Varda Bar-Kar told me that, for her, "there has to be something in it that is some kind of contribution to humanity." Along the same lines, producer Gill Holland said, "I try to do films with social, moral underpinnings that try to change the world." That is what resonates with them, and you get to choose something that resonates with you. Finding meaning in your work is key. Dimitri Logothetis advises, "Don't do something because someone tells you to do it. Do it because you believe in it."

Every successful producer finds a coping mechanism to manage the stress and rejection. For instance, Chuck West told me, "I walk my faith, live my faith, and everything happens for a reason." You can only build a successful filmmaking career if you are true to yourself, and go about your work fueled by passion and tenacity.

Blockchain, Crypto, and NFTs Might Matter, Someday

In all of my interviews, no one brought up an experience financing a film on a blockchain, with a crypto currency, or through the use of non-fungible tokens (NFTs). These might be viable fundraising tools in the future, but right now, they are not helping get independent films made on a large scale. The learning curve on all of these new technologies is steep, there are not a ton of competent consultants who can help you navigate them, and I'm afraid it will be a waste of your time to try to fund your movie with them. Therefore, I am not prepared to encourage you to explore them for your film today. Ask me again in five years.

The Craft of Filmmaking Matters

> If your content is good, you will find the right partners.
> – Chevy K. Chen, producer

This book is really finance-oriented intentionally. I've been a participant or audience member in so many discussions about independent film finance over the years that focus on the quality of the film, and not finance. I trust that you already know that the quality of the script really matters and the quality of the production really matters. This is certainly not the place for me to tell you how to craft a good script or improve your production quality, but I want to assure you that you must be able to do both to be a successful producer. That said, I want to share this one amazing quote from *Pete's Dragon* writer Toby Halbrooks: "if you can't tell if your thing is good or not, it's not."

In your role as a producer, Julie Lynn stresses that "you must develop your own taste, commit to it, and develop a reputation for it." Greg Lauritano similarly will advise you that "your taste in material is really important." Matthew Parker warns, "don't pick something that sucks." Many producers suggest that aspiring filmmakers keep watching movies, reading scripts, and getting picky. In Mr. Lauritano's words, "Having other people understand that, if you choose something, they're going to respect that this isn't the first thing that you've read. You've read 100 scripts, and this is the one thing you picked."

Also note that your taste does not need to be genre-specific to build a successful career. Cybill Lui Eppich noted that "it's fun to use different parts of my brain." She added that having a diverse pipeline means that you "don't have to pitch one versus the other." Likewise, Carly Hugo recommends that producers "do both docs and narratives," to help grow your skillset and career. If a big television network or streaming platform is funding the documentary, it can even pay you better than a narrative feature. Josh Penn agrees. He says doing both "keeps me sane, because I'm in much more control of the fate of my documentary projects."

I was surprised at how few of my interview subjects worked on-set or as a line producer before beginning to make their own films. I can share a couple of conflicting opinions here. On one hand, Nicholas Tabarrok argued that the skillset of a line producer is substantially different than the skillset of a creative or financial producer and is not a terribly helpful foundation to a producing career. And he should know – he worked as a line producer on several projects.

On the other hand, Joel Shapiro, producer of *Dear Dictator*, recommends that you "absolutely understand how the hot dog is made – spend the time working all of the departments." That is precisely what he did, as he transitioned from a career in investment banking to his new life as an independent producer. Talk about getting your hands dirty - Mr. Shapiro did garbage clean-up, catering, grip, electric, locations, transportation, and lots of other jobs on set to learn how movies are made. He relies on that on-set experience to know where he can trim budgets but still preserve the quality of the film. His time on set also lets him understand the culture of the departments, and how to prevent expensive problems before they arise.

Notes

1 Please don't drink and drive.
2 This book is a product of warm introductions, as one producer would introduce me to another. Special thanks to my aunt Jacqueline Schenkein, whose warm introduction to her distant cousin, Brad Zions, led to a chain of an additional seven amazing warm introductions.

18 Action Plan

> Make movies, then go out and make new movies.
> – Maximilian Leo, producer

There is a lot of advice in this book about how to finance your film and grow your career from successful producers. All of it may seem overwhelming at this point. In this chapter, I will do my best to break it into a few simple actions that you can focus your energy on to keep moving forward.

Write a Business Plan

In order to attract investors, you need a business plan for your film that clearly maps out the First Law of Film Finance. This includes building a credible estimate for the market value of your film and a financing plan. Be sure to include your budget top sheet too. In my experience, if you work on it daily, it will take you at least a month to get your business plan to a place where both the content and the presentation format are ready for primetime. If you wait until a potential investor asks you for a business plan to get started on your first draft, then you are too late.

Build Your Professional Network

It is essential that you continue meeting new people and strengthening your existing relationships. Worry less about how these meetings can benefit you today, and focus more on the long-term potential. The important thing is to find people that you share common interests with and enjoy being around. Those are the comrades who will want to go along on a crazy journey with you. There are so many roles involved in making a single movie, and it is best to have friends that you like filling all of them.

Keep Working

The work experience that you gain today gives you credibility, teaches you new skills, and lets you meet other working professionals.

(The paycheck also lets you finance your own development.) Make an effort to reflect on what you learned each day, and how it can be used to make you a successful producer. View every day on the job as another important step towards getting your film financed.

Keep Learning

There are so many great books, podcasts, trade publications, and live events to learn from. I named some of my favorites throughout the pages of this book, and put them all in the appendix, but I encourage you to follow your curiosity and find your own too. Think like a student – take notes in one notebook or file, and review them weekly. The great thing about independent film producers, as evidenced by all of the wonderful folks that sat for interviews with me, is that they love to mentor and give back. Accept any generosity that is offered to you.

Make Your Movie

Do it! Go make your movie! Make a difference. Make us laugh. Make us cry. Make money for your investors. And then make another, and another, and another. I hope that you build a successful career!

The End

Appendix
Additional Resources

> Did you read the book?!
>
> – Lawrence Offenberg, father

Books

To understand the investor's perspective:
Cohen, Joseph N. *Investing in Movies: Strategies for Investors and Producers.* Routledge, 2017.

A classic book to understand participations:
Daniels, Bill, David Leedy, Steven D. Sills, and Peter Klass. *Movie money: Understanding Hollywood's (Creative) Accounting Practices.* Silman-James Press, 2020.

Particularly for documentarians:
Dean, Carole Lee. *The Art of Film Funding.* Michael Wiese Productions, 2012.

For help writing your business plan:
Levison, Louise. *Filmmakers and Financing: Business Plans for Independents.* Routledge, 2016.

For advice on how to approach investors:
Malloy, Tom. *Bankroll. A New Approach to Feature Film Financing.* Michael Wiese Productions, 2012.

The classic legal tome:
Moore, Schuyler M. *The Biz: The Basic Business, Legal, and Financial Aspects of the Film Industry.* Silman-James Press, 2018.

A great collection of essays by industry professionals and studio executives:
Squire, Jason. *The Movie Business Book.* Routledge, 2016.

Appendix

To understand how films make money:
Ulin, Jeff. *The Business of Media Distribution: Monetizing Film, TV and Video Content in an Online World*. Routledge, 2019.

If you want to go deep into the economics:
Vogel, Harold L. *Entertainment Industry Economics: A Guide for Financial Analysis*. Cambridge University Press, 2020.

Podcasts

"The Business," hosted by Kim Masters.
"Indie Film Hustle," hosted by Alex Ferrari.
"Strictly Business," hosted by *Variety*.
"The Town," hosted by Matthew Belloni.

Trade Publications

Deadline's business section: https://deadline.com/v/business/
Hollywood Reporter's business section: https://www.hollywoodreporter.com/c/business/
IndieWire: https://www.indiewire.com/c/film/
Screen Daily: https://www.screendaily.com/news/funding
Variety: https://variety.com/v/film/
The Wrap: https://www.thewrap.com/category/movies/

Glossary

Above-the-line The writers, producers, director, and leading cast.
Advance rate A percentage of the Minimum Guarantee's value, reflecting the maximum loan amount that a lender is willing to extend to a borrower.
AFM American Film Market.
Ancillary revenue Money earned based on the intellectual property of the film, not the distribution of the film, such as licensing revenue and sequel revenue.
Asset Tangible and intangible things that have value to a business, including cash, cameras, trucks, and intellectual property.
Below-the-line Everything in the budget that is not Above-the-line.
Box office receipts The sum of all money paid for tickets at the theater to see a specific motion picture.
Cash The sum of all physical currency and money in the film's bank account.
Cash-flowing Term used to describe a company's use of cash-on-hand to pay all costs of making the film, as those costs happen.
Collateral Property that a lender can legally seize to help pay off a loan if the borrower does not voluntarily pay.
Collection account manager A third-party that receives all revenue earned by a movie, and then pays it out to parties according to the terms of the Collection Account Management Agreement (CAMA).
Common stock A financial instrument indicating ownership of equity in a corporation.
Comps Previously released films that are substantially similar to the proposed project. Also known as Comparables or Comparable Films.
Completion bond A contract that guarantees that the film will be delivered as specified in other contracts with distributors or financiers.
Costs Money spent by an organization to run its operations. Also called expenses.
Debt Money that is owed to another party, usually requiring interest to be paid too.
Deferment see Deferral.

Glossary

Deferral Compensation that will be paid once a certain goal has been reached.

DGA Director's Guild of America.

Distribution The process of monetizing the finished film through theatrical release, as well as releases on other platforms and media.

Distribution rights A contract that allows a party to sell copies of a film within predetermined windows in a specific territory.

Distributor A company that either sells the rights across various windows to exhibit the film or exhibits the film to audiences itself, such as a streaming service.

EFM European Film Market.

Equity (independent film definition) An investment position typically consisting of both a loan to be repaid with a premium and a share of the profits. The loan is higher in the Waterfall.

Equity (traditional definition) The portion of the assets that belong to the owners of the firm after they pay their liabilities.

Exhibitor A company that provides access to the finished film to consumers. Examples include theaters, streaming services, and pay television providers.

Expenses See Costs.

Financier Any person or company who provides cash, goods, or services to a film in exchange for a debt or equity ownership stake.

Gap loan A loan that is issued based on the expectation of future sales of a film's distribution rights in one or more territories.

Intellectual property The creative parts of a film or other work that is unique and innovative, including the story, dialogue, characters, props and locations.

Interest Money paid over time for the use of another party's money.

Investor see Financier.

IP see Intellectual Property.

Liabilities Amounts that the business is required to pay in the future, including loans, deferrals, and credit card bills.

Line producer Person responsible for managing the budget, while also in charge of all operations for a film from pre-production through post-production.

LLC Limited liability company.

Loan Agreement to borrow money that requires the borrower to repay the lender the amount borrowed plus interest at some point in the future.

Minimum guarantee A fixed amount of cash paid to the producers by the distributor when the completed film is delivered to the distributor.

Negative pickup An agreement in which a single distributor agrees to pay for the entire production cost of the film, payable once the film is completed.

On spec Act of making a movie without any signed distribution contracts.

Overage Money earned according to the terms of a contract in excess of a minimum guarantee or advance.
P&A Prints and advertising, but more recently repurposed to publicity and advertising (i.e. marketing).
Participation A contract providing a share of the profits earned by the film, if any.
Point 1% of the profits of the film.
Presale A contract providing distribution rights for a specific film to a distributor before production of the film has begun, in exchange for a minimum guarantee plus overages, if any.
Profits Revenue minus all expenses.
Return The repayment of money originally invested (also known as principal) with interest.
Revenue Money earned by an organization through sale of its goods and services related to its operations.
SAG-AFTRA Screen Actors Guild and the American Federation of Television and Radio Artists. The labor union representing on-screen talent.
Sales agent A party responsible for licensing the film's distribution rights to distributors around the world.
Sample A population involved in a research study that is smaller than the entire population.
Share A unit of common stock in a company.
Spec see On Spec.
Stock The equity in a publicly traded company. Often called common stock.
Talent agent A person or corporation who engages in the occupation of procuring, offering, promising or attempting to procure employment or engagements for an artist or artists.
Tax credit A rule issued by a government allowing for a reduction of the income taxes that a party is obligated to pay the government.
Tax incentive A rule issued by a government allowing for a reduction of the taxes that a party is obligated to pay or providing compensation to the party based on the spending by the party within the government's jurisdiction.
Vig Interest earned on an investment.
Waterfall A financial statement showing the order and amount parties are to be paid by revenue earned from a movie.
WGA Writers Guild of America.
Window A method for distributing a film. Also known as a Release Window.
Windowing A process of releasing a film through various windows, typically in sequence, one at a time, from the highest-value consumers (theatrical) to the lowest-value consumers (free television and streaming services).

Index

Page numbers in italics refer to figures. Page numbers in bold refer to tables. Page numbers followed by 'n' refer to notes.

$0 assumption approach 91–92
"120 and 50, The " 34, 118; see also equity

A24 14–15
Academy of Motion Picture Arts and Sciences 176
accountant 54, 174
accounting 25, 27, 37
account manager 22, 41, 114; see also collection account manager
action plan 179–180
actors' values 104
ad-supported streaming services 19
advance rate 42
advertisers 128–129
Albert Nobbs 151
Amazon Prime 15, 160
Amazon Studios 14
American Film Institute 153–154
American Film Market (AFM) 21, 41, 47, 104–105
American Psycho 86
America Online 150
ancillary revenue 90
Anderson, Wes 15
angel investor events 163
Annapurna Pictures 15, 128
AppleTV+ 15
April 29, 1992 160
Ara, Tom 102
Arthur Vining Davis Foundation 68
assets 16, 26–31, 33–34, 40, 93, 162
associate producer 9, 11
Athenaeum Theatre in Melbourne 19

attorneys 18, 171–172
Avengers: End Game 23n1, 50, 64
Avengers: Infinity War 23n1, 64

Back to the Future II 54
Back to the Future III 54
balance sheet 26–28, 34, 114
Baldecchi, John 128, 133, 149
bank/banking 29; and accounting 173–174; transaction costs 42; see also lender
Bank of America 173
Bar-Kar, Varda 176
Barnum, Robert 150
Batgirl 100
Beasts of the Southern Wild 43–44, 164
Beaudoin, Tony 47
Beckmann, Brian 136
Bergman, Ram 23
Berlinale Co-Production Market 159
Besson, Luc 39
best-case scenario bias 99
Betamax 19
Bezos, Jeff 16
billboard ads 22
Billingsley, Peter 112–113
Birthday Cake, The 86
Bixby, Lauren 165
Biz, The 79
Blackfish 13
Black Panther 61
Blockbuster Video 32, 167–168
blockchain 177
Bloom 21

Blum, Jason 154
Blumhouse Productions 154
bonds, insurance and deposits 75–77
Borderline 160
borrowing money 42–43
box office: receipts 9, 22, 94–95; revenue 22
Boyhood 53–54
Bread and Butter 151
bridge: lenders 46; loans 40, 45
broad comps 95–102
budgets 86–87, 89, 118; bonds, insurance and deposits 75–77; contingency 75–76; first film 72–75
Bullock, Sandra 50, 118
Burns, Todd 69, 162
Business of Media Distribution, The 22
business plan 110, 171, 179
Butan, Marc 18, 130
Butler, Gerard 69
Butterfly Effect, The 151

California credits 64
California Film Commission 64
Cannes 21, 41, 104
capital 31, 79
Caplan, Seth 73
career: making independent films 17; stability 23; success 37
cash 38n1; -flow independent producers 78; -flowing 78; line 40
cash-on-cash return 120–122
Catalyst 159
Catapult Film Fund 68
Chakraborty, Milan 95, 135–136
Chappelle, Dave 56
Chappelle's Show 56
Cherry 105
cherry-picking narrow comps 94–95
Chinese Theater 160
Christmas Story, A 13, 112–113
CineMart 159
cinematographer 54, 102
Clerks 92
Coda 99
cold call 173
collateral property 40–41

collection account manager 22, 41, 113–114, 116, 140, 175
completion bond 42, 58, 73, 75–76, 86, 117
comps: analysis for a script 96, **97**; "black swan"-type 94; broad 95–102; cherry-pick narrow 94–95; narrow 92–95
contingency 75–76
control over project 175
co-producer 9, 11
corporate finance 37
corridor 125n4
costs 25–29
COVID 55, 94, 165
craft of filmmaking 177–178
Creative Artists Agency (CAA) 18
creative pitches 170
credit/credibility 151, 154; cards 31; as director 9
crowdfunding 69, 79
Crowe, Russell 20
crypto currency 177

Daniels, Bill 59
Dark Knight, The 62
Da Vinci, Leonardo 134–135
Davis, Viola 96
Day to Die, A 135–136
Dear Dictator 112, 178
debt financing 27, 40–48
deferments *see* deferrals
deferrals 57–58, 118
DeLorean 31
Despres, Naomi 144, 158, 165, 175
Dieppa, Felipe 18
digital download 19
Disney 14–15, 31; film 54; stock 31
Disney+/Hulu 15
distribution 14, 19–22; platform 9; rights 21, 41, 78–79, 89, 97, 112, 160
distributors 18–23, 41–45, 75, 78, 98, 102, 104–105, 114–117, 123, 129, 132, 134, 174
dividend 30–31
Dix, A.J. 18, 151, 153, 168–169
documentaries 13; filmmaking 154–155; producers 9

Index

Documentary Producers Alliance (DPA) 76
Dog, Snoop 134
donors and passionate advocates 162
Dora the Explorer 18
DreamWorks Animation 22–23
Dual 98, 101
DVD 9, 19, 32

economy/economic 15; indicators 31; power 16
Einbinder, Scott 150
El Mariachi 92
Emmerich, Roland 46
Empire Strikes Back, The 40
entertainment attorney 21, 57, 172
Entourage 105
Eppich, Cybill Lui 174–175, 177–178
equity 26–37, 59, 133–138; in age of streaming 142–143; debt and 30; -financed films 17, 47; financiers 69, 119, 121, 123, 130; in independent film 31, 33–36, 127–144; investment 129; investors 30–33, 51–52, 118, 127–128, *128*, 130, 132, 136, 159; *vs.* liabilities 33; -like contract 59; Netflix 30; in real world 36–37; sources 36
Estonia (*Tenet*) 62
ethnic or racial identity 12
European Film Market (EFM) 21, 104, 159
Everything Everywhere All At Once 15
executive producer 9, 11
exhibitors 21

Fadida, Maurice 150, 160, 168
Fassbender, Michael 57
film: budget 74–75; commissioners 159; LucasFilm 22–23; Marvel film 78; Natalie Portman film 57; R-rated 50
Film Independent (Fast Track) 68–69, 159
Film school 11–12

finance/financial: crisis 150; distress 15; financial wisdom 12; investments 127; landmarks 58; tool for domestic narrative producers 9
financiers 9, 18, 43, 50, 53–54, 57, 68–69, 74, 80, 86, 94, 105, 108, 119, 123, 134, 154, 174
financing plan 29, 85, 87, 89, 110, *111*, 118–120, 132; estimating returns 119–124; market value and, sample comparison *112*; mitigate the risk 112–113; sample returns table **125**; sources *152*; stack 31; waterfall 114–118, **115**
Fintage House 114, 125n3, 175
"first dollar gross" participation deal 118
First Law of Film Finance 85–88, 110, 119, 132, 138, 171, 179
fiscal sponsor 68–69
Flatland 73
Fleabag: The Scriptures 22–23
Fleischman, Eric 74, 138, 154
Flower 138
foreign distributors 129
foreign exchange (FX) 113
Fosheim, Ricky 21, 136
Fox 31, 40
France, Lisa 70
Freeway 114, 125n3, 175
academic degrees 11–12
Furious 7 76–77

Gabrawy, Mike 16–17, 161
gap loans 40, 44–45, 117–118
Georgia vs. World 64–67
Gesualdo, Cathy 175
Get on the Bus 134
Get Out 94
Gibler, Stephen 151
Gibson, Mel 50
Girl in the Photographs, The 166
Global Road 15
Glory at Sea 43
Gone with the Wind 54
Goodfellas 56
Goodman-Bhyat, Zaheer 150, 162
Gosling, Ryan 20

Gotham Film and Media Institute, The 159
Gotham Week Project Market 159
grants 67–69
Gravity 50, 118
Green Book 129
Green Knight, The 172
gross profits 51
Groundhog Day 170
Grow House 134

Habitat for Humanity 87
Halbrooks, Toby 157, 172, 177
Harvey, Andrew 128
HBO Max 15, 56
Head Hunter, The 21
hedge funds 129
Hello Sunshine 15
Hideaway Entertainment, The 165–166
high-net-worth individuals 36, 128, 130–131, 134–136
hits-driven business 17
Holdovers, The 96
Holland, Gill 74, 172, 176
"Hollywood Accounting" 55–57
Hollywood machinery 18
Hollywood Reporter, The 14, 20
Hotel Mumbai 16–17
Houten, Andrew van den 132, 135–136
Hughes, Howard 127
Hugo, Carly 178
Huston, John 150
Hype 155

IMDB 37, 48, 49n5, 174
Inception 62
income statement 25–28, 34, 50, 114
Inconvenient Truth, An 13, 129
independent producers 11, 16–17
independent productions 174; companies 129–130; economics 16–17
independent studios 15–16
Indian Paintbrush 15
"Indie Film Hustle" 20
IndieWire 97–98
informational interview 173

institutional equity investments 37
institutional investors 129
insurance companies 129
intellectual property (IP) 14, 16, 22–23
interest 29–35, 56, 117, 140; -free loan 57; origination fees 42; rates 32, 42
internal rate of return (IRR) 120, 122–123
International Film Festival Rotterdam (IFFR) 159
investments 29; equity 129; finance/financial 127; institutional equity 37; riskier 31; safer 31
investors 143–144, 171; pitches 170; profit participation for 52
iTunes 19

Jane Got a Gun 57–58
Jenkins, Patty 167–168
Jerry Maguire 133–134
Johnson, Rian 23
Judas and the Black Messiah 129

Keeyes, Jon 162
Kicking and Screaming 154
Killing Them Softly 18
Kill the Messenger 144, 158
Klass, Peter 59
Knives Out 23, 119
Korenberg, Rosanne 4, 159

language of business: accounting 25; equity 29–37; income statement 25–26; *see also* equity
Lauritano, Greg 177
law degrees 11–12
lawyers 159
leaps of faith 138–139
Leedy, David 59
lender 16, 31, 40–41, 46, 159; blacklist 41–42; bridge 46; interest rates and origination fees 42; mezz 47, 116–118; non-bank 41; tax credit 63–64
Leo, Maximilian 10, 37, 48, 176
Levine, Matt 29
liabilities 26–29, 33, 59

Liberated 69
lifetime box office 9, 37, 48, 152, 155n, 174
limited liability corporation (LLC) 14
Linde, David 129
line producer 74–75, 86, 108, 111, 113, 164, 171, 178
Linklater, Richard 53–54
loans 40, 45, 113
local filmmaker events 161–162
local TV ads 20
Lopez, Jennifer 58
Los Angeles (LA) 174–175
Louie, Mynette 157
Lucas, George 40
LucasFilm 22–23
luck 167–169
Lynn, Julie 151, 177

MacDonald, Bill 134, 150
Machine Gun Preacher 69
Mahoney, Thomas 153–154, 166
Mainstream 74
major studios 14–15, 130
Mann, Thomas 46, 171
Margin Call 74
Mark, Laurence 133–134
market value 85, 87, 118–119; $0 assumption approach 91–92; broad comps 95–102; budget 89; financing plan 89; narrow comps 92–95; prepare to pivot 108; producer estimates 106–108; revenue 89; sales estimates 102–106
Martin, Steve 154
Marvel 15, 78
MBA 11–12
McNulty, Tom 156–157
median budget 151–152
Mexican, The 133–134, 149
mezzanine loans 40, 45
mezz lender 47, 117–118
Microsoft 31
Midway 46
Minding the Gap 67
minimum guarantees 41, 117
Monster 167–168
Moonfall 46

Moore, Schuyler 79
moral burden of equity 139–142
Motel 7
Motion Picture Association (MPA) 14
movie business: distribution 14, 19–22; independent producers 16–17; independent studios 15–16; intellectual property (IP) 22–23; major studios 14–15; production business 14–18; profit motive 13; talent agencies 17–18; theaters 16; *see also* independent producers
"*Movie Business Book, The* " 18
Movie Money: Understanding Hollywood's (Creative) Accounting Practices 59
Murphy, Cillian 103
Murphy, Eddie 23
Musk, Elon 16
mutual funds 29
My Friend Dahmer 95

Nanny 97–98
narrow comps 92–95
Nash, Bruce 37, 48
negative pickup loans 40–41
Neon 15
Netflix 14–15, 19–20, 23, 54–56, 65, 69, 103; balance sheet 33; equity 30; stock 31–32, 120
Netherlands (*Dunkirk*) 62
net profits 51
networking 106; and angel investor events 163; events 161; breakfasts, lunches, and happy hours 162; churches and charities 162; film markets, festivals, and premieres 158–160; film school and business school 157–158; grocery stores 163; on job 158; local filmmaker events 161–162; nonspecific networking and angel investor events 163
New Mexico (*Oppenheimer*) 62
Nice Guys 20–21
Nike 128–129
Nolan, Christopher 62, 96

non-bank lenders 41
non-fungible tokens (NFTs) 177
nonmonetary returns 33
non-profit organization 68
non-refundable non-transferable tax credit 67

Oberman, Siena 74, 86, 105
One of the Hollywood Ten 67
on-screen: stars 18; talent 73
Oscar nominations 12, 44, 67
ownership stake 30–31

Paramount 14–15
Paramount Global 26, 41, 56
Paranormal Activity 92, 94, 154
Parasite 94
pari passu 58
Parker, Matthew 18, 43, 177
Parker, Trey 25–26
Participant Media 129
participation 50–60, 80, 118, 121–122
Pasquino, Alessandra 176
Passion of the Christ, The 50, 59
Payne, Alexander 96
Payne, Judd 80, 105
Peacock (Universal) 15
Peaky Blinders 103
Pecorin, Clay 46, 87
Penn, Josh 43, 159, 164, 178
pension funds 129
Pepsi 128–129
perpetual contract 54
personal income statement 25
personal networks 36–37
Peterson, Clark 167
Pete's Dragon 177
Phok, Peter 17, 156
physical currency 38n1
physical media 20
Pinewood Atlanta Studios 64
pipelines 164–166
piracy 24n3
pitches 170–171
Pitt, Brad 133
Plane 130
Plus One 135
Points on the Backend 51

Pollard, Stu 85–86
Portman, Natalie 57
Pray, Doug 154–155
presales: contract 80; loans 40–42, 116–117; and tax incentives 138
price discrimination 19–20principal photography 41
priority 31, 114–119
private equity funds 129
producers 8–9, 113; careers snapshot 10; estimates 106–108; experienced 43; personal networks 37
"Producers Sustainability Survey Report" 12, 55
production: accountants 54, 113; business 14–18; SAG-AFTRA production 77; unit production manager 54; *see also* independent productions
profit 28–29; motive 13; negative 26
profit participation: compensation form 53; deferrals are not 57–59; for investors 52; payment 52; perpetual contract 54; for talent 52–55; for you 55
pro-rata 58
Prototype 154
Purge, The 116
Putman, Ross 131

Queen of the Desert 66
Queen's Gambit, The 103
Quon, Diane 67

Ramsay, Lynne 57
Raslan, Nick 66
rebate 66
Redbox 19, 32
refundable tax credit 66
regression analysis 38n3, 49n5
Relativity Media 15
repetition 29, 29
returns estimation 119–124; cash-on-cash return 119–122; internal rate of return (IRR) 120, 121–123; sample returns table **125**; sharing 124; *see also* cash-on-cash return

Revenant, The 75
revenues 25–26, 28–29, 89, 125n4
Rhodes, Matthew 165–166
risk 32; mitigation devices 113
Risk-Return Tradeoff 31–33
Roberts, Julia 133
Roll with Me 70
"Rule of Three" 15
Rule of Thumb 103
Russo, Joe 23n1

Sackman, Jeff 86, 88, 160
SAG-AFTRA production 77
sales estimates 102–106; actors' values 104; agencies 132; agents 22, 102, 116; over time 104; social moods change 104; stars 103
Sands International Film Festival of St. Andrews 23n1
saving 29
scarcity 16–17
senior notes 31
Shapiro, Joel 112
shares of stock 30
Silencing, The 174–175
Sills, Steven D. 59
Sisters 175
Skoll, Jeffrey 129
Sleight 154
sliding-scale costs 73
Smith, Kevin 92
social media 22
soft money 61, 69–71
Sony Pictures 14–15
South Park 25–26, 41
Spicer, Nick 96
stars: -owned business 129; sales estimates 103
Star Wars 23, 49n2
stock 30
Stone, Matt 25–26
Stoning of Soraya M, The 69
Story of the Kelly Gang, The 19
Stowaway 10, 46, 96
Stranger Things 30
streaming: platforms 16; services 9, 21
stress tolerance 176–177

Summit Entertainment 15
Sundance Film Festival 100
survivorship bias 99

Tabarrok, Nicholas 7, 158
Tale, The 157
talent: agencies 17–18; agent 17, 108, 170; compensation 27; -focused production companies 15; and investors 57
Tamasco, Jason 144, 150–151
tax credit 61–67, 112; lenders 63–64; payment 117
Taxi Driver Test 10–11
tax incentives 45–46, 61–66, 79, 90–91; funds 64; loans 40, 45–46, 117; money 63
Taylor-Joy, Anya 103
Telescene 7
television channels 16
theater owners 21, 22
theatrical release 9
Theron, Charlize 153, 167–168
Tonya 159
Toronto International Film Festival (TIFF) 21
traditional windowing strategy 19–20
transaction costs 42–43
transferable tax credit 66–67
Tuchinsky, Jessica 18
TV channels 21
Twilight 15

Ulin, Jeffrey 22
ultimate revenue 90
United States Bureau of Economic Analysis 62
United States Federal Reserve Survey of Consumer Finances 73
unit production manager 54
Universal Pictures 14–15, 76–77
unpaid expenses 114
U.S.-based producers 9

Valerian and the City of a Thousand Planets 39
Veltri, Scott 158, 172
VHS 9, 19

ViacomCBS 26
visual effects animators 13

Walker, Paul 76–77
Walking Dead, The 50
Waller-Bridge, Phoebe 22
Wallis, Quvenzhané 44
Wall Street-type entities 129
Walt Disney Company 78
warm introduction 173
Warner Bros 14–15, 21, 100
waterfall 114–118, **115**
wealthy investors 134–135; *see also* high-net-worth individuals
West, Chuck 158, 176–177
Who Framed Roger Rabbit? 54
Wild Indian 153–154
windowing strategy 19–20
windows 19
Winkler, Irwin 56

Witherspoon, Reese 15
Wizard of Oz, The 19, 54
Wolf, Jonathon 21
Wolofsky, Lisa 116
Women Make Movies 69
Wonder Woman 167
work experience 179–180
worldwide distribution rights 97–98
worldwide revenue 37
worse-case value 100
worst-case scenario 100
writers 13

Yang, Janet 2, 176
"Young Fresh Fellows" 155
youth 172–173

Zeitlin, Benh 43
Zions, Brad 150
Zuckerberg, Mark 16

For Product Safety Concerns and Information please contact our EU
representative GPSR@taylorandfrancis.com
Taylor & Francis Verlag GmbH, Kaufingerstraße 24, 80331 München, Germany

www.ingramcontent.com/pod-product-compliance
Lightning Source LLC
Chambersburg PA
CBHW051358290426
44108CB00015B/2062